a blessing to so
many families!

Get ALL Fired Up!

About Living Your

Dreams

REVISED EDITION

Published by Al Duncan Publishing LLC
www.alduncanpublishing.com

Library of Congress Cataloging-in-Publication Data

Duncan, Al
Get all fired up! about living your dreams/ by Al Duncan — Revised Edition
p. cm
Includes bibliographical references.

ISBN13: 978-0-9831900-1-1
LCCN: 2011900158

1. Personal Development. 2. Self-Help. 3. Self-Improvement
4. Teenagers. 5. Young Adults.
I. Title

Cover Design: SS Media, Inc.

To Pamela Duncan, my mother,
for sacrificing her dreams so that her
six children would have a chance to live theirs.

Contents

The Enemy Within

"Man, I can't go out like this. I need to do more. Before I leave this planet I gotta make an impact on this world."

"Oh yeah? How are you going to do that? You can't even impact your own life the right way."

"Doesn't matter what happened. Ain't no excuses. Starting right now, I'm about to make a difference. I'm about to speak life to young people. They feel my story. I'm about to help empower them just like I helped Nate and those other young guys."

"Are you kidding me?! Everybody has a story, bro'. And besides, that was different. That's your little brother. You don't know the first thing about talking to young people. You're a professional chef. Stick to the kitchen, buddy."

"That's not really my thing. I did that to take care of Nate. I'm tired of it. I used to be a professional saxophone player. I know how to rock the crowd. I got stage presence and a message."

"Whatever! That was different. You didn't have to talk that much. Nobody even cared if you could talk. Do you think you're going to get up in front of a room full of people? You ain't even got good English skills."

"Then I'll get better."

"But nobody knows you."

"But they will soon."

"How?"

"I'll get a TV show..."

"You?! Al Duncan? On TV? Man, please. You are seriously trippin'."

"Maybe I'll write book or something."

"You ain't got no computer. You don't even know how to type!"

"Then I'll learn."

"You know you done lost your mind, right? Get on back in that kitchen."

"Look, man, you might as well shut up because there is no way I'm going to let you or anything else stop me. I'm about to help millions and make millions so go ahead and watch. And keep watching. And while you're watching I'll be working on my dreams."

–A conversation between the "old me" and the "new me" in July 2000

Duncan Nugget #11
You are guaranteed to win once you defeat the enemy within because...
It's ALL Mental!

I.
One Word, Mixed Messages

Dreams. How can one little word fill the world with so much joy and pain? It gives birth to hope and despair. It brings peace of mind and confusion. That one little word is full of mixed messages.

Dreams cause some people to jump up and down with unbridled enthusiasm while shouting, *"This is amazing! I can't believe this is happening!"* That same word, however, causes other people to curse their life in frustration, knowing that they could have accomplished a lot more.

Dreams can fill some hearts with congratulations, admiration, and awe. But that same word fills the hearts of others with vicious criticism, contempt, and envy.

Dreams will have some people doing things they didn't think they could do. It will have others doing things they shouldn't do!

Is anything more exciting than your wildest dreams come true? Is anything more frustrating than the dream that got away? Is anything more disappointing than hoping that something happens, it finally does, and then you realize that it wasn't all you dreamed it would be?

Duncan Nugget #314
People are praised for attaining
their dreams, but often ridiculed
for chasing them.

Think about that. It's crazy. It makes absolutely no sense.

If you spend too much of your time daydreaming then they say *"you're lazy"*. They tell you to *"get your head out of the clouds"*.

If you spend too little time going after your dreams then they say things like *"you lack ambition"* or *"you're a coward"*. If you don't dream at all then *"you don't have any imagination"*.

If you come up with a big idea for a new invention or starting a multi-million dollar company then somebody will probably hit you over the head with the phrase *"only in your dreams!"*

On the other hand, if you're doing something amazing (that they never believed you could do in the first place) then they say, *"You're living a life most people can only dream about."*

Dreams. There is no escaping that word. It's the subject matter of movies, TV shows, songs, fairy tales, and of course, this book. From the womb to the tomb, dreams—fulfilled and unfulfilled— are an integral part of our lives.

Duncan Nugget #315
Dreams—all children have them;
not enough adults live them.

Million-Dollar Question:
What happens in between?

The typical answer is: life happens.

Garbage.

It's your life. Fix it...if you want to.

Duncan Nugget #316
I would rather die
in pursuit of my dreams
than live the perfect nightmare.

If this is your first book on living your dreams then I hope that you will be inspired and encouraged to begin living the life you deserve. If you are already living your dreams or if you've already read a book or two on the subject then maybe by the time you finish this book you will find the last number to the secret combination that will unlock the next level of happiness and fulfillment for you.

ARE YOU IN LOVE?

Warning: This book is full of hot and steamy love affairs. Not the kind you find in romance novels. I am talking about the love affairs between people and their passions. The people that you will learn from in this book wake up every day and do what they love to do. In chapter 8, Chanell St. Junious—successful attorney, poet, and Desert Storm veteran—says that as a child she developed "a love affair with words."

How many people do you know that are absolutely in love with their profession? You may have to make sacrifices and do things you would rather not do along the way, but you should ultimately end up loving your life.

THE DIFFERENCE BETWEEN MISERY AND HAPPINESS

I know quite a few miserable poor people and quite a few miserable rich people. I also know quite a few happy poor people and quite a few happy rich people. Obviously, it's not the money that separated the two groups.

It's fulfillment.

Whether it is time freedom, financial freedom, the joy of being of service to another human being, or all three, the people you are about to hear from are happy. That's priceless. All of them are rich where it counts—inside. That's a dream come true.

MORE THAN ONE WAY

As you read the Duncan Nuggets™, articles, and interviews in this book, you will discover insightful answers to questions like:

✓ How can a person be okay with failing when failing can feel so humiliating?

✓ What advice would you give someone that is interested in turning his or her passion into a profession?

✓ How did you figure out what you were supposed to be doing in life?

✓ How did you know when it was time to start pursing your dreams?

✓ What did you do to make it through the tough times?

The answers to those questions show that I and the people you will hear from in this book have similar philosophies about many things. There are some things, however, about which we disagree. For example, in their articles on goal-setting one of my mentors, Dr. Kevin Hogan, and a good friend of mine, Dr. Joe Teal completely disagree about the usefulness of the phrase "*A goal is a dream (wish) with a deadline*". Yet and still, both of them are successful.

I asked everyone that I interviewed for this book whether or not they had any regrets. I asked them if there was one thing that they could change about their lives what would it be? Once again, all of them didn't agree. Some don't believe in regrets. Others do have things that they regret or things they would've done differently. Nevertheless, the one thing that everyone you'll hear from has in common is that there came a point in time when we chose to get all fired up about living our dreams. As a result, we've experienced a great deal of abundance and happiness.

What's the lesson in this? Take the information and inspiration you get from this book and carve your own path.

Duncan Nugget #114
There is no full-proof, guaranteed way
of becoming successful in life. You are
not looking for who's right and who's wrong.
You are looking for what works.
More specifically, you are looking
for what works for YOU.

The Whisper

"It's freezing out here!"

The frost-bitten voice of my girlfriend snapped me back into reality. It was an icy-cold, bone-chilling day in "da 'Burgh"—Pittsburgh, Pennsylvania. I was sitting outside in my favorite chair. The few belongings that I had left were scattered all around me. As I sadly looked back at my apartment building—a place I called home just a few hours earlier—I felt the pain of the skin-cutting winter wind blowing across my face. My girlfriend continued with the verbal beat down.

"How could you let this happen?! Are you just going to sit there like that? I know you are going to do something about this, right?" She was furious.

I fired back, "Please, baby, please! I'm trying to think." She ignored me and kept right on fussing.

"Wah, wah, wah, wah..."

She was starting to sound like the teacher from Charlie Brown. As her voice faded into the background, the voice in my head got louder.

"This sucks!"

I sat there thinking that it couldn't get any worse and then it started to snow! Outwardly, I wasn't moving a muscle. Internally, there was a lot going on. One part of me was complaining and blaming everyone and everything else except for myself. Another part of me—a penetrating whisper—was not letting me off the hook.

"It's my girl, man. I should've got with somebody with money..."

"Huh?! So, now you're a child? You need your mommy to pay your bills?"

"It was my parents. They...they got divorced...they didn't teach me about money..."

"Garbage. You knew better than to spend all of your money on stupidness."

"It was my dad, man. He was smokin' crack. That ruined my life..."

"Ruined YOUR life? Really? He's already getting his life back together. What's your excuse?"

"But I was molested at five..."

"Look, you've already dealt with that. And anyway what does that have to do with you paying rent?"

"It was my roommates. They left me hangin'..."

"You knew they were shady when you met them."

"I should've never left Philly. It's society, man! They don't want a young brother like me to have anything."

"Oh, now this has something to do with your skin color? You weren't sayin' that while you were makin' and blowin' all of that money playin' your sax."

"It's...it's..."

"It's you, man. It's you."

—Al Duncan sitting curb side, Pittsburgh, PA 1995

Duncan Nugget #111
Regardless of your age, race, gender, or circumstances there are two words that will carry you to success:
No Excuses.

As an entrepreneur and a musician I've been dead broke too many times to count. Learning how to deal with and overcome financial challenges is a part of being successful in life. But the challenges I was experiencing when I was sitting curb side in "da 'Burgh" were the result of 100% pure, unadulterated stupidity.

That wasn't the only time I screwed everything up. I've made a ridiculous amount of mistakes and wasted a ton of time. To me, that's not a badge of honor. It's the truth—real talk.

I still make a lot of mistakes, but not as stupid as the ones I made back then. A big part of the difference boils down to two words: **No Excuses.**

Duncan Nugget #112
No matter what happens in your life, refuse to blame anyone or anything else. Period. Just get to work on making things better.

CHANGING PEOPLE & BEING IN CONTROL

But all of this isn't my fault. I didn't ask for this to happen.

Although I agree with that statement, it still doesn't change anything, does it? If you take the stance that your mess is someone else's fault, then you are in trouble.

Why? Because you cannot change other people.

Duncan Nugget #121
Change yourself.
Forget about changing other people.
You can't really change other people.
You can influence them, but it's up to them
to make the change. Your precious time
is better spent focusing on two things you
can change: your attitude and your actions.

In other words, if you're waiting for someone else to change so that you can make your life better, you are completely wasting your time. Time that you could be using to work on your dreams.

The same thing goes for situations that are beyond your control. Why? Because you can't control everything and it's a total waste of your time to worry about things beyond your control.

In other words, *it's not what happens. It's what you think and do about what happens.* All of this boils down to your Power of Choice.

Duncan Nugget #110
You can make an excuse or you can make a
way, but... you can't do both.

I would love to be able to tell you that after that day—sitting in my favorite chair in the snow—a miraculous change occurred, but that's not quite how it happened. Reaching your dreams doesn't usually work that way.

I didn't realize it until years later, but the day I got evicted, a seed was planted. Every time I screwed up and refused to make any excuses about what happened, I was watering and fertilizing that seed. I was protecting and growing my dreams.

DREAM SLAYERS

excuse (ĭk-skyūs′) n. 1. An explanation offered to justify or obtain forgiveness. 2. An explanation offered to justify an action or make it better understood. 3. An inferior example: a sorry excuse for a car. *4. dream slayer.*

Duncan Nugget #109
Excuses are Dream Slayers.
They have killed more dreams than anything else in the history of the world.

You have to protect your dreams from excuses. Every time I encounter a dead dream a "perfectly good" excuse is somewhere near by. (If you know of something that has slain more dreams than excuses have, please fee free to let me know.)

There's an excuse born every millisecond. They come in all shapes, sizes, and colors. Here are some of the most popular ones (listed in no particular order).

29 Popular Excuses and A Few Words About Them

1. I'm not old enough.

How old are you? Regardless of the number that just popped into your head, there is someone on this planet in the same age range as you who has experienced a great deal of success. So can you. Think about:

- ✓ Mark Zuckerberg—founder of Facebook, became a billionaire in his 20's.
- ✓ Farrah Gray—became a millionaire business man by the age of 14.

✓ Booker T. Washington—founded Tuskegee University when he was 24.

✓ Raven-Symoné—has been a superstar actress since she was 4 years old.

✓ Juliette Brindak—founded her company, Miss O and Friends, at 10. Her company was worth $15 million by the time she was 19.

✓ Bill Gates—founded Microsoft when he was 19 years old.

If you can't think of anybody else, go to my website and contact me. I'll send you some more examples. www.alduncan.net

2. I'm too old.

See #1 and #3

3. It's too late.

Are you still breathing? Colonel Sanders didn't create the Kentucky Fried Chicken (KFC) franchises until he was 65. Gandhi didn't start his non-violent civil disobedience movement until he was in his 40's. Rosa Parks was 42 when she refused to give up her seat on the bus.

If you can't think of anybody else, go to my website and contact me. I'll send you some more examples. www.alduncan.net

4. I'm the wrong race or ethnicity.

Are you kidding me?!

We now have an African-American President of the United States. Do I really need to say anything else? Of course, prejudice and discrimination still exist. Regardless of your race or gender, however, there are people just like you who have created great lives for themselves. Join them.

If you can't think of anybody else, go to my website and contact me. I'll send you some more examples. www.alduncan.net

5. I'm afraid/nervous/worried.

Duncan Nugget #163
The difference between a hero
and a coward is not the lack of fear.
It's the lack of action.

You must refuse to allow fear to stop you from living your dreams. We'll spend sometime talking about fear in chapter 4. Also, in my book, **My Success Journal For Young People (3rd Edition)**, there is a good exercise on conquering your fears.

6. I don't have the money.

That's exactly why you should want to work on your dreams—because you don't have the money. Get it? If not, think about it for a minute. How are you ever going to stop being broke?

Do you know how many poor and down-trodden individuals have gone on to live the life of their dreams? MILLIONS.

Lack of money is no excuse. In fact, for many successful people, the lack of money was one of the driving forces behind their success.

7. I don't have the resources.

Well, work on getting them! Or get with somebody or some organization that does. See #6, #8, and #9.

8. I didn't/don't know.

Then find out. It's not really all that complicated. Ask somebody. Get a mentor, a tutor, a coach, or a friend. Just make sure he or she has the right info or knows the right thing to do. If that doesn't work, there's this little thing that some genius invented. You're using it now. It's called a book. And some other genius invented something else. It's called the internet. Use it.

9. I'm not good enough.

Get better.

Or partner up with someone who is good enough.

This is another time when you want a mentor, a tutor, a coach, or a friend. Just make sure he or she knows how to help you do whatever needs to get done. Maybe this is a good time to delegate. Who told you that you have to do everything yourself?

10. I'm not attractive enough.

Are you serious?!

Have you ever seen Flavor Flav or Mic Jagger? If not, go Google them. Not sexy. At all. You might not be ready to be a model, but you'll feel a whole lot better about what you see in the mirror. (Yes, my mother told me not to talk about people.)

If you feel overweight or too skinny, then how about working out? It'll make you feel better.

Warning: Be careful about trying to live up to someone else's standard of beauty. If you are feeling depressed about the way you look, get some help now. Seriously—talk to somebody about it, okay? Regardless of your body type or physical limitations there is someone on the planet like you who has experienced a great deal of success.

11. I'm too fat.

How about a career as a Sumo Wrestler? Ha!

But seriously, you need to work on this one for the sake of your good health. You don't have to be skinny. Just be healthy, okay?

Think about Monique and Gabriel Iglesias (famous comedians). Think about offensive linemen in the NFL. Also, there are ton (pun intended) of plus-size models that are very successful. I personally know plenty of business owners and CEO's that are overweight and that hasn't stopped them.

See the last paragraph of #10

12. I'm too skinny or scrawny.

Think about me, Al Duncan. I used to be able to hide behind a pole. I still might be able to.

See the last paragraph of #10

13. I'm too short.

Think about Mini-Me from Austin Powers, or the Lollipop Kids from the Wizard of Oz! Okay, okay...I know you don't want to be the Lollipop Kids.

Here are some better examples:

✓ Spud Web (the 5'7" Slam Dunk Champ)
✓ Mary Lou Retton (the 4'9" gold medal gymnast)
✓ Beethoven (the 5' 3" German composer and pianist)

See the last paragraph of #10

14. I'm too tall.

But think about how much easier it'll be for you to change a light bulb!

Here are two good examples:

✓ Lisa Leslie (6' 5") is a former professional women's basketball player. She is a two-time WNBA champion, a three-time WNBA MVP, and a four-time Olympic gold medal winner. Can you imagine being a 12-year old girl and the tallest person in your school? (She was 6' 1" in middle school.) That had to be tough.

✓ At 6' 4", Abraham Lincoln, considered by many people to be the greatest U.S. president, was often described as lanky and kind of awkward.

See the last paragraph of #10

15. I'm not fast enough.

Then you're perfect for a job with the government. They're always moving slow!

Think about the story of The Tortoise and The Hare. If you don't know it, find it and read it. It's a priceless lesson. Sometimes, it's not about being the fastest. It's about being the most consistent.

Also, there are oodles of successful athletes that were considered to be slow. For example, Larry Bird was named one of the 50 greatest NBA players.

See the last paragraph of #10

16. I'm not talented enough.

When is the last time you saw a bad actor in a blockbuster movie? When is the last time you heard a hit song on the radio by someone who couldn't sing or rap? Haven't you ever heard someone say that she is smarter or more talented than her boss or teachers?

There are a lot of average people living their dreams and plenty of "talented" people who are starving artists. Think about that.

Lack of talent is no excuse. Just look at the early rounds of American Idol. Ha!

(But don't get me wrong. I have a ton of respect for those fallen American Idol contestants. At least they have heart. A chance to fall flat on your face in front of millions would make most people too afraid to go after their dreams.)

See #5

17. It's too hard.

If it were easy then wouldn't everybody be doing it? And then it wouldn't much of a dream, would it? When you are passionate about something and you love to do it, it might be hard, but it's worth it.

18. I'm too tired.

Too tired of working on your dreams?! How about being tired of not having enough money? What about being tired of being unhappy and unsatisfied? How about being tired of being tired?

Work on living your dreams and you will have a lot more control over your life. Then you can be too tired from doing things you love to do.

19. It's too much work.

Too much work? Then you have the wrong dreams. You're supposed to love working on your dreams. Can you imagine Will Smith saying that acting is too much work? He would say it's challenging, but the words, "too much work" would never come out of his mouth.

Keep in mind that work ethic is a vital key to goal achievement. Whatever you do requires a great deal of effort to master. In his book, Outliers, Malcolm Gladwell writes about research that shows that it takes 10,000 hours to master something. In that case, you better love what you want to master. It's a lot of work, but it shouldn't be too much work.

There's a common expression that goes something like this: *"Love it so much that you would do it for free, but do it so well that they pay you!"*

20. That's not my thing.

Then stop what you're doing right now and go find something that is your thing. In the words of the Isley Brothers: *"It's your thing. Do what you wanna do."*

Also, I've seen a lot of people say things like:

"School ain't my thing."

"Math ain't my thing."

"Reading ain't my thing."

Garbage.

You already know the importance of knowledge or you wouldn't be reading this book. But let's pretend you didn't.

How are you supposed to get the knowledge you need to succeed if school or reading "ain't your thing"? How are you supposed to manage all of that money you want to make if "math ain't your thing"?

You don't have to be a brainiac, but having the right knowledge is crucial to your success. This is the Information Age. The right info has to be a steady part of your diet. It's the key to self-development.

Be a life-long learner.

21. It's impossible.

Do you mean like:

✓ Winning a golf tournament on a broken leg? (Tiger Woods)
✓ Writing 12 books even though you are deaf and blind? (Helen Keller)
✓ Graduating from college at 10? (Michael Kearney)
✓ Teaching yourself how to read? (Frederick Douglass)

✓ Being a homeless junkie at 17, getting your life together, and becoming the owner of a company with $26 million in sales? (Bob Williamson)

Have you ever noticed that a lot of times when one person says something is impossible, a little while later someone else is doing it? Have you ever noticed that a lot of times, when one person thinks an idea won't make money, a little while later someone else is making millions off of it?

There are tons and tons of people who have done the impossible. You should join them.

22. I have kids.

Their kids are the reason that many successful people do what they do. For two interesting perspectives on working on your dreams while raising children, read my conversations with Alix Graham-Michel and Chanell St. Junious in chapters 7 and 8.

23. My parents suck.

Okay. This is a tough one. But it's still no excuse. There are millions of successful people with lame parents. If your parents are abusive then get some help now. **Nobody can stop you.**

See #8 and #9.

(By the way, how do you know that you're not the one being lame? Parents complain just as much about their children as children do about their parents.)

24. My teachers suck.

This is tough one, too. The same thing applies: There are millions of successful people with lame teachers. Get some help. Talk to somebody. There is NEVER a good reason to give up on school. **Nobody can stop you.**

See #8 and #9.

(By the way, how do you know that you're not being a lame student? Teachers complain just as much about their students as students do about their teachers.)

25. My boyfriend/husband or girlfriend/wife sucks.

This is another tough one and once again, it's no excuse. There are millions of successful people with lame ex's. Notice that I said "ex's". If a person is holding you back or causing you a lot of pain and suffering it's time to move on. **Nobody can stop you.**

(For the last time, how do you know that you're not the one being lame? Women complain just as much about men as men do about women.)

26. I have to go to work.

It is frustrating dealing with a boss you can't stand and a job you don't like. If that's you, then I guess you better get to work on your dreams, huh? As long as you're not a lame employee, this should be fuel, not an excuse. There are millions of successful people who had lame jobs and bosses.

This work thing can be tricky, however, when you don't really hate your job or your boss. You're not miserable or happy, just kind of blah. The word is: complacent. It's hard to change when you are comfortable.

I've been in this situation before so, I feel you. You gotta make money, right? You have bills to pay, things to do, and it's hard to make time. True. But you probably still find time for TV, talking on the phone, or playing around on the internet, don't you? Hmm...

First, you need to decide whether or not you really want to change your situation. Then *see #28 and #29* for your excuse about not having time.

27. If God wanted it to happen then it would've happened.

Can you say "free will" and "muscles"? How about using them? You cannot sit around doing nothing.

There is no great individual from any religion that got away with doing absolutely nothing. No action, no accomplishments. Do nothing if you want to, but somebody else will be living your dreams.

28. It's not the right time.

This is a tricky one because timing is crucial to success. It's good to have patience. A lot of people, however, say that the timing isn't right because of fear. Then they use patience as a way to hide their fear and "not the right time" becomes another pitiful excuse to do nothing. Think about that. Is that you?

If it's not now, exactly when is the right time? You never know. So, you want to be thoroughly prepared and ready to seize every opportunity. That means you have to keep striving.

If you need help see #8 and #9.

29. I don't have the time.

Oh, yeah. I forgot. Successful people actually have 36 hours in a day, right?

Garbage.

You can't add hours to your day. Just get better at using the ones you have. Wake up an hour earlier or go to bed an hour later. That's an extra 30 hours per month to work on your dreams. It's 60 hours per month if you do both.

Is your sleep too precious? Then spend an hour less per day watching TV, talking on the phone, or playing around on the internet. That's another 30 hours per month. Take an hour away from all three and that's an extra 90 hours per month.

Do everything I've suggested here and you'll have an extra 150 hours per month to work on your dreams. That's almost a whole week. You have time. How you use it is up to you.

From billionaires to broke folk, everybody has 168 hours in a week. That's it. People are always talking about "trying to find the time." It's not a question of finding time. Here's an excerpt

from a series of articles I wrote titled "*A State of Mind Called Time*":

> *What we're going to talk about has nothing to do with time management in the popular sense. This is all about your perception of time. The way you treat and think about time.*
>
> *Most people are always trying to find time. But the thing is, it's impossible to find time. It doesn't work that way.*
>
> *You can find your keys. You can walk down the street and find some money. But you can't walk down the street and find an hour. You don't go to the lost and found when you've lost precious time.*
>
> ### You do not find time; you make time.
>
> Read the rest of the article and the entire series here:
> www.alduncan.net/time.html

THE NITTY-GRITTY

Here's the nitty-gritty about excuses in three words:

Blame is lame.

Constantly making excuses and playing the blame game is a pathetic, feeble way of life. It leaves a person practically powerless to do anything about anything. Remember:

Duncan Nugget #110
You can make an excuse or you can make a way, but... you can't do both.

Faith

I was walking through our living room headed to my home office when I caught a glimpse of a talk show that my wife was watching. I couldn't believe my eyes.

I asked Renee, "Did I just see what I think I saw?" With a look of astonishment on her face she replied, "Yeah!"

What I saw was a two-legged dog walking upright like a human! I know what you're thinking and I was thinking the same thing when I saw it.

WHAT?!

The dog is named Faith. Faith was born with only one front leg, which was severely deformed. Eventually, because of atrophy, that leg was removed. The talk show host asked the owner how she was able to teach Faith to walk upright. The owner said the first thing she had to do was get Faith to believe that it was possible.

That's right. Even dogs have to believe it before they can be it.

This whole thing blew my mind. I kept thinking the same thing over and over again. "No excuses. If a two-legged dog can learn to walk upright, you have no excuses, man. No excuses." I was also thinking, "Now that's what you call real dogged determination!" The lesson here is even in the dog world...It's ALL mental!

—Excerpt from e-zine article
www.alduncan.net

III.
Constant Elevation

Dream achievement is really a three-step process. It's not complicated, but for some reason people tend to make it complicated. I call this three-step process Constant Elevation.

Constant Elevation is the continuous pursuit of more and better.

I'm talking about more happiness, more satisfaction, more achievement, more fulfillment, and whatever else you want more of in your life.

I'm talking about a better life, better friends, a better environment, better skills, and whatever else you want to be better in your life.

The steps for Constant Elevation are simple:

Learn. Do. Improve.

LEARN – GET THE RIGHT INFO

"Why do I have to learn this? This is a total waste of time. I'm never going to use this stuff."

Have you ever heard somebody say that? I used to make that complaint all the time. A lot of people make that complaint. In some cases, it's a legitimate complaint. But you know what's funny?

When most people graduate from school they start spending the a lot of their time learning all kinds of stuff that won't help them get where they want to go in life.

Think about it. They learn things like:

✓ What happened on their favorite TV show
✓ The words to the hottest new song
✓ The latest gossip at school or work
✓ Who won the game
✓ The latest dance moves
✓ The cheat codes to a new video game

There's nothing wrong, per se, about learning these things. Entertainment is a good thing—in moderation. But do you spend more time learning that type of information as opposed to the type of info that moves you closer to your dreams?

Million-Dollar Question:
What will I learn today and how can I use it to accomplish my goals and live my dreams?

I'm not saying that you have to become a walking Wikipedia. Enjoy life. Learning about your passion and what it takes to be successful should be fun and interesting.

Continue to read books like this, listen to audio programs, take classes, and go to seminars. Watch DVD's or online videos about your dreams. Check out some documentaries and biographies and get to know people who do what you want to do.

While you are seeking information, however, know this:

Duncan Nugget #99
There is a lot more information than there is truth.

Today, we have more experts than ever, but we still have more problems than ever. Isn't there something wrong with that picture? Make sure your info is coming from a good, reputable source. And...

Just because you heard it on the news or found it on the internet doesn't automatically make it the truth.

Wrong info will dry up your cash flow, ruin your credit, and destroy relationships. Plus, you'll spend a boatload of time unlearning what you learned. So, be thorough, consistent, and diligent in your search for knowledge. Get the right info.

DO – USE WHAT YOU LEARN

You're learning right now while reading this book. So, what are you going to *do* with that you're learning?

"Doing" is the fuel that makes your dream machine go.

You can learn how to build a pyramid, but unless you do something with your knowledge there will be no pyramid.

Learning something that can help you and not doing anything with the knowledge is DUMB.

I don't care if that sounds harsh. It's real talk. But I don't want to offend anybody so, let's see if I can say it in a nicer way.

Duncan Nugget #135
Constantly letting your hard earned
knowledge go to waste is
a guaranteed way to end up
P.I.C.—President of the Idiot Club.

Well...at least that way is funnier!

Do I always use what I learn? No. And when I don't, I remind myself about how dumb it is to do that. I am no longer P.I.C. I'm much better at using my knowledge than I used to be. That's one of the main reasons that I'm a lot more successful than I used to be.

As soon as you learn (or remember) something useful you've got to ask yourself: **How am I going to use this?** For instance, sooner or later you might read something in this book that you already know (maybe you already have) and when you do, the question that will immediately pop into your head is:

"I might know that, but how am I using it?"

If you read something new then the thought that will pop into you mind is:

"Now that I know that, how can I use it?"

In other words, no matter what you come across in this book or during your pursuit of knowledge, if it can help you, you will be using it.

For many folks, the gap between what they do and what they know is a black hole. Their dreams are lost in that black hole because they spend years in school, get plenty of knowledge from various sources, and do nothing with what they have learned.

P.I.C.

That's not cool.

Duncan Nugget #19
The gap between what you know and what you do is crucial to your success Most people aren't unsuccessful because they don't know what to do. They are unsuccessful because they don't DO what they know how to do. Knowledge is power IF...you use it!

IMPROVE – GET BETTER

No matter what's going on in life, the most advantageous thing to do is to improve. Even if you're already experiencing success getting better is a good idea.

Get better at helping other people.

Get better at communicating.

Get better at being a student.

Get better at being a parent.

Get better at taking care of YOU.

Whatever it is...

Get better.

If you don't like where you are in life then you need to understand that in order for things to improve you must continue to get better. There are all kinds of obstacles that people allow to keep them from getting better. The three that I focus on in this book are fear, other people, and complacency. We'll talk about fear in the next chapter.

OTHER PEOPLE

Two of the biggest challenges you'll face while working on your dreams are: other people's opinions and other people's problems. These two challenges will ruin you if you allow them to.

Duncan Nugget #40
A person's definition of you does not define you.

Never settle for somebody's opinion about what you can and cannot do. You must refuse to allow anyone to keep you from improving. No exceptions. If you allow somebody else to keep you from getting better, you're P.I.C. (Ouch! Sometimes the truth hurts.)

I had straight A's my first year in high school. I was one of the top students in my class. That same year, my parents got divorced and I found out that my childhood hero—my father— was addicted to crack cocaine. That was a tough period in my life. I let the problems around me keep me from getting better. By the time I graduated from high school I was one of the worst students in my class. P.I.C. I learned a valuable lesson from that experience.

Duncan Nugget #208
Never let somebody else's mess get in the way of your success.

Note: Today, my father is clean. He's gotten his life back together and he's one of my closest friends. ☺ Failure is only permanent if you quit.

COMPLACENCY

I touched on this in Excuse #26 in the previous chapter, but let's dig into it a little bit deeper.

You don't have to settle for your life the way it is if you really want it to be better.

That seems like basic common sense to me. Unfortunately, however, most people do settle. They are complacent. You're not surprised by that, are you? After all, it seems like an easy, hassle free way of living. Just be happy and grateful for what you already have, right? Eh...not quite.

There's a thin line between happiness and complacency.

When you accomplish your goals, be happy. You earned it. There's nothing wrong with being satisfied and you should always be grateful for what you have.

If you have enough money to make you happy and you don't want any more, that's cool. If you feel like you have a nice enough car and a big enough house, that's cool. You define success however you define success. I just want it to last once you have it.

If you're not careful, complacency can cause success to slip through your fingers.

Complacency is the dark side of happiness. It's not just being satisfied. It's being too satisfied. It's being willingly stuck where you are in life and unconcerned about it.

Duncan Nugget #116
Complacency robs the world of
a person's true potential.

Rarely, do I come across a successful person that is complacent. They may be happy and satisfied, but not complacent. If things are great in one area of their lives, they're working on getting better in another area. When I do run into a successful person that is complacent, normally, later on down the road they are experiencing some difficulties that could've been avoided.

Complacency is like carbon-monoxide. It's odorless and colorless. It poisons a person's drive and determination without the victim realizing what happened.

The only thing that clears the air of complacency is the desire to improve.

Get Better.

FOCUS ON YOUR STRENGTHS

When you encounter obstacles and make mistakes the only thing you can do to stop the cycle from repeating forever is to get better. You've got to improve. It's all about becoming a better you.

Figure out what you're strengths are and hone them until they are razor sharp.

Notice that I didn't say "work on your weaknesses."

It's much more effective and encouraging to figure out what's right with you instead of spending all of your time worrying about what's wrong with you.

That doesn't mean you should ignore your weaknesses. Get help with them or get somebody else to deal with them. For example, get a tutor to help you in math or get an accountant to do your taxes then you can spend more time getting better at whatever you do best.

Duncan Nugget #47
Spend some of your time focusing on your weaknesses; spend MOST of your time focusing on your strengths.
In other words, focus more on what you CAN do and focus less on what you can't do.
Remember... It's not a question of "what's wrong with you?"

Million-Dollar Question:
What's RIGHT with you?

WARNING

These three steps for Constant Elevation are so simple that a lot of people usually gloss over them. That's a terrible idea. A good *learn-do-improve* routine will help you stay strong and steady on the path to living your dreams. Constant Elevation will keep stumbling blocks and setbacks from becoming permanent.

IV.
Energized!
How to Stay Fired Up Forever

Imagine a time when you were excited. I'm talking about a time when you were fired up! In terms of energy, the time I want you to think about has to be a time when on a scale of 1 to 10, you were at a 10. Think about a time like that.

Got it?

Once you have that time in mind, slowly start to turn your level 10 energy up to a 12. How does that feel?

Let's turn it up more...to a 15! By now you are feeling extremely energized—extra fired up! Holler out loud (or in your head),"I'm fired up!" Say it again. "I'm fired up!" Now say, "Watch out—somebody might get burned!" Ha!

If you followed my instructions, you're feeling pretty good right now but, what happens later on or tomorrow?

Getting fired up is easy. Staying fired up is HARD.

Have you ever been feeling like "rah, rah, rah," highly motivated to get something done and a little while later your motivation and energy have completely disappeared?

Or have you come home from a long day knowing there are some things you need to work on to help you become successful, but you don't feel like doing it?

Why does this happen?

What happens to your energy?

Accomplishing your goals and achieving your dreams is impossible without a tremendous amount of energy. You've got to be fired up and energized. Even when you love what you do, every now and then it's hard to get yourself fired up.

Million-Dollar Question:
How do you get the energy to do what you need to do when you don't feel like doing anything?

You will find the answer to that question in the following story.

The Clueless Driver

Once upon a time in a city called Stupidity, there was this guy driving down the highway. He was speeding away when he suddenly noticed flashing lights in his rearview mirror. Guess who.

A cop?

Exactly.

So, Clueless—that's what everybody called him—pulls over. The officer walks up to the window and taps on it. Clueless rolls down his window and the officer asks, "Sir, did you know that you were going 75 in a 55?"

"Actually, officer, I didn't know that. How was I supposed to know?"

The officer gave Clueless a strange look and asked, "Sir, have you been drinking? You don't know how tell how fast you were going?"

"No, officer, how am I supposed to know?"

In an extremely sarcastic voice the officer said, "There's a little thing in your car called a dashboard and on your dashboard there's an odometer. That's the thing with numbers on it that tells you how fast you're going. You should try using it some time."

In a surprised and stupid voice, Clueless responds, "Ohhh… Is that what that's for? Thanks, officer, I've never even bothered to look at that thing before."

The officer was so confused and astonished by Clueless's response that instead of a ticket, he only gave Clueless a warning and they both drove off.

A little while later and further down the road, Clueless began to notice something strange going on with his car. It started to sputter and shake. Then it just cut off. Clueless coasted to the side of the road, got out of the car, and slammed the door closed. He started hollering at the car and kicking it. He was so enraged that he didn't even notice the officer who pulled him over earlier, driving up behind him.

The officer got out his patrol car and asked, "What seems to be the problem, sir?"

A bit startled, but still irritated, Clueless responded, "I don't know what's wrong with this stupid car. It's brand new. I just got it today."

The officer said, "Tell you what, get back in the car, try to start it up and let's see if we can figure out what's going on."

"Okay." Clueless tried to start the car. Nothing happened.

"You have got to be kidding me," said the officer who was looking inside in the car. "Sir, there is nothing wrong with your car except for one thing: You're out of gas!"

"I'm out of gas? Aw, man! How was I supposed to know that?"

"You really are clueless aren't you?"

"Of course I am. That's what everybody calls me."

"You know that thing I told you about earlier?"

"The dashboard?"

"It has something on it called a fuel gage. It tells you how much gas you have in your tank," explained the officer while shaking his head in disbelief.

"Thanks officer! From now on, I'll make sure I look at the dashboard. Now...can you help me find some gas?!"

_____

HOW OFTEN DO YOU LOOK AT YOUR DASHBOARD?

Before you can answer the question about finding the energy when you don't feel like doing something, you have to answer this question:

Have I been speeding through life without checking my personal dashboard and keeping an eye on my fuel gage?

"There is more to life than just increasing its speed."

Those are the words of Mahatma Gandhi. Most people are moving so fast in life that they barely have time to pay attention to what's really going on with them. They are stressed out (money and people problems), worn-out (job, school, homework, and studying), burnt-out (frustrated, overworked and underpaid), and zoned out (too much TV, radio, video games, internet, drugs and alcohol). All of that adds up to a lack of energy, which means many people don't even feel like working on their dreams.

Duncan Nugget #238
Human beings don't work like cars. If a car only has a quarter of a tank of gas the car will still function normally, but if you are operating on a quarter-tank of energy you will not be your normal self. That is why you have to constantly keep you eye on your fuel gauge and consistently fill your tank.

There really isn't a magic trick for staying energized and fired up. It boils down to paying closer attention to your life and what's going on in it. You have to look at the dashboard and keep your eye on the gage.

Be on the lookout for the things that will help you stay energized and avoid the things that waste your energy.

THE ROOT OF ACTION

When you finally decide to do something what is it that causes you to do it? What causes a person to take action?

I've asked thousands of people at hundreds of speaking engagements those two questions. I get answers like: something negative, motivation, a desire, frustration, fear, and love. While all of these are correct to some degree, the answer is much simpler.

Duncan Nugget #63
Action is determined by importance.

Action is based on what's most important to you at a specific moment in time.

It doesn't matter if it's negative or positive; conscious or unconscious, it's a lot easier to stay energized and fired up when something important happens.

It's not necessarily the action itself that is important to you. In fact, you might not even like what you're doing. For example, plenty of students talk to me about how they "can't stand school" but, they go because they know that school will allow them to attain many of the things in life that are important to them.

(Of course, some students don't feel like going and just go because it's more important not to get in trouble!)

Here's another example. Let's say that you come home from a long day. You finally get a chance to sit down and you're thinking to yourself, "there is no way I'm moving. I am not doing anything else today. I'm just going to sit here and chillax. Bedsides, I don't have the energy to move even if I wanted to." Have you ever had a day like that?

So, you're sitting there and all of sudden the phone rings. You answer the phone and it's someone close to you and they are having an emergency. The next thing you know, you've jumped up and you're headed out the door.

Where did that energy come from? Hmm...

What if the phone rang and instead of it being bad news it was some good news?

Someone is on the phone telling that you that you have just won the lottery and you have 30 minutes to come pick up your money. After you check your caller id and see that this is a real call from the state lottery, would you make it to where you need to be in a half-hour? For a million dollars?! Of course you would. You might make it in 5 minutes, right? And you would have all kinds of energy, wouldn't you?

Where did the energy come from?

It came from inside of you. Out of nowhere, something that was very important to you came into play, you got a boost of energy (maybe it was adrenaline), and you went to handle your business.

Duncan Nugget #64
The way you get
yourself to do something
even when you don't feel like it
is to create a strong
bond between what you
need to get done and
something that is extremely
important to you.

Think about it. How many times have you been dead tired, but you had some work to do? It could've been work for class, your job, or community service. Unless the work was due the next day, you probably decided that you were too tired to do it that night. Instead, you figured that you would finish it later. But if whatever you were working on was due the next day, then although you were dead tired, you probably still managed to find the energy to get it done.

Thirty days before a project is due, sleep may be more important but, the night before who cares about sleep? You're work is more important at that point in time. It's urgent.

The trick is learning how to keep what is only important in the moment from causing problems with the things that are REALLY important in the long run.

Here's a series questions that I got from one of my mentors, Kevin Hogan. He uses them as a selling technique, but they are perfect for helping you determine what's most important to you. It's best to answer them in writing. So, grab a piece of paper and get busy. (If you own a copy of my book called *My Success Journal—For Young People* use some blank pages in it for this exercise.)

1. **What's most important to me about school?** (NOTE: You can take out the word "school" and put any scenario, situation, object, or person in its place. For example: life, friends, work, girlfriend, or success.)

2. **How do I know when I have it [answer from #1]?** (You can also use this question: What does [answer from #1] mean to me?)

3. **Is there anything more important than that?** (If yes, then identify what it is and answer questions 2 and 3 again. Repeat this until you get to the absolute most important thing.)

Once you have the answers to those questions then whenever you don't feel like doing something that's important you can ask yourself the following question:

Million-Dollar Question:

How is _____[scenario I don't feel like dealing with or action I don't feel like doing] going to help me get/be/feel _____[any of the things that are most important to me]?

(If you're confused by how this works, don't worry. I'll give you an example below.)

The answer to that final question will either a) give you some stronger reasons to do the important things that you are reluctant to do or b) help keep you from wasting your energy on things that won't have a positive impact on your life.

Here's how a young entrepreneur that was procrastinating about doing his business plan completed the exercise during one of my workshops.

What's Most Important?

What's most important to me about my business?

Answer: Being Successful

How do I know when I am successful or what makes me feel successful?

Answer: Being good at what I do and making enough money to pay my bills and saving some money to invest.

So, when I am good at what I do and I make enough money to pay my bills and I'm saving money to invest, I feel successful. As far as my business is concerned, once I am successful is there anything more important than that?

Answer: Yes. I have to be happy.

How do I know when I am happy?

Answer: When I feel good and proud about what I do and when I have a family to share all of my success with.

So, when I feel successful and I feel good and proud about what I do and I have a family to share my success with I'll be happy. As far as my business is concerned, once I'm successful and happy, is there anything more important?

Answer: Yes. I wouldn't feel right unless I was there for my grandma because when my parents died she took care of me.

What does "being there for my grandma" mean?

Answer: It means being there to take care of her when she needs me.

So, once I feel successful and happy and I know that I'm there for my grandma is there anything more important than that?

Answer: No.

How is finishing my biz plan going to help me be successful, happy, and take care of my grandma?

Answer: My finished biz plan will keep me focused and help me understand what it is going to take to run a business which is what I need to be successful, happy, and take care of my grandma.

KICK PROCRASTINATION TO THE CURB

What causes procrastination?

If you were to ask a random group of people that question these are some of the answers you would get:

✓ Laziness
✓ Anxiety
✓ It's painful

✓ I just don't feel like doing it.

✓ I don't want to step out of my comfort zone.

✓ I'm not sure if I can really do it.

✓ I hate doing that.

✓ This isn't fun.

✓ This is boring.

✓ It's too hard.

✓ It won't make a difference anyway.

All of those answers boil down to two main things that cause people to procrastinate:

Fear and Aversion

If you want to kick procrastination to the curb you have to conquer fear and aversion. It's okay if you are a little nervous or afraid of taking the steps necessary to accomplish your goals. It's okay if you hate to do some of the important things that will carry you to success. But...

It's NOT okay to let fear and aversion stop you.

Here's a declaration that will help you if your procrastination is being caused by fear:

I'm afraid/worried/nervous about doing this, but that's okay because once I do it then I can have/do/feel_____[whatever is most important to you] and I refuse to allow anything to keep from _____ [whatever is most important to you].

Here's a declaration that will help you if your procrastination is being caused by aversion:

I don't want to do this (or I don't feel like doing this), but that's okay because once I do it then I can have/do/feel _____[whatever is most impor-tant to you] and I refuse to allow anything to keep from _____ [whatever is most important to you].

Sometimes you have to say these declarations over and over and over again to yourself until you start to believe them. It's not always easy. For example, I love speaking, but writing isn't always fun for me. If I'm not careful I will procrastinate like crazy when it comes to writing books and articles. I have to constantly remind myself before I get started and while I'm writing that the books and articles are ways for me to help people, like you, empower themselves. I also have to keep saying to myself over and over again that books and articles are a great way for me to make money to take care of my family.

My declaration looks like this:

I don't feel like writing, but that's okay because once I finish what I'm writing I can use the book or article to empower some young people, provide for my family, and feel like I've done something worthwhile with my life. I refuse to allow anything to keep me from doing that.

You have to find something or someone so important in your life that you are willing to feel the fear and aversion and still do what you need to do. That's why it's crucial that you do the exercise from earlier.

What's most important to you?

_____

_____

Conquer Fear

Fear is one the most powerful forces governing our behavior. It is the feeling of being threatened by something physically (a gun), mentally (a test), or emotionally (he might leave me). Regardless of whether the threat is real (a hungry bear) or imagined (what if everybody laughs at me?) your body initially responds the same way—you go into flight or fight mode.

When your body fears for its physical, mental, or emotional safety it decides action is required. It's time run or rumble. If somebody yells, "watch out!" it is fear that causes you to move out of the way just in time. Without fear, the piano that they were moving probably would've landed on your head instead of on the ground.

As you can probably tell, the purpose of fear is to protect you from harm. This means that fear, like all emotions, starts with good intentions. But have you ever heard the expression "the road to hell is paved with good intentions"? You can put yourself through hell if you allow your fear to run amuck. Untamed fear will wreak havoc on dreams, goals, plans, and ideas. Fear, unconquered, can erode self-confidence, self-worth, self-esteem, and self-motivation. So, if you want to be successful, your fear must be identified and conquered.

A lot of people are like me. I get nervous, but I don't show that I'm nervous. Where I come from (North Philly), it's not cool to show fear. It's considered to be a sign of weakness. They say it makes you look like a punk, a chump, or a coward. Maybe you agree with all of that, maybe you don't, but one thing is for sure—being nervous or afraid is NOT the sign of a coward.

"The hero and the coward both feel the same thing, but the hero uses his fear, projects it onto his opponent, while the coward runs. It's the same thing, fear, but it's what you do with it that matters."
—Cus D'Amato (Boxing Trainer)

—Excerpt from
My Success Journal For Young People (3rd Edition)
By Al Duncan

RESISTANCE

Someone emailed me the following question:

"Why is it so easy to muster up the strength and energy for unimportant situations (petty arguments) and not for situations that are very important (maintaining

health or acquiring wealth)? It seems as if people have little or no energy for what's most important."

That is an excellent question. Here's part of my response:

A: It boils down to one word: Resistance.

Human Beings and electricity have something in common. Both seek the path of least resistance. That's the reason that we invent so many gizmos—to make life easier and less resistant. And that's the reason that it seems as if it's easier to muster up more energy for less important tasks.

It takes a lot more discipline (resistance) to manage your emotions and properly channel them. Allowing your emotions to run wild—like screaming and yelling at someone—wastes a great deal of energy and time but PERCEPTUALLY there's little resistance because it seems easier than practicing restraint.

Think about how hard it is to resist "snapping on" somebody that you think did something stupid. Or what about how hard it is to resist getting in to an argument when someone is making a statement that you don't agree with. Internally you have to resist the urge to interrupt. It takes great discipline to actually listen to what the other person has to say, make sure that you understand and respect what they have to say, and then state your point of view.

How about this one? "I'm too tired to exercise for an hour today." And then the person ends up hanging out with a friend until the wee hours of the morning. Which one wasted more energy? Which one presented more resistance?

Here's another one. "I'm too tired to cook tonight. I'll just get something from the drive thru." So, you do and

you save some time and energy, right? But the fast food is harder on your system, it takes more time and energy to digest, and you body gets less energy (nutrition) in return. So, which one wasted more energy? Which one presented more resistance?

Last example: Ever notice that reading is a great sleeping pill for most people? Two or three paragraphs and it's a first round knockout. But that same person can stay up, watch TV half the night and then go to work on a few hours of sleep. Wasted energy? More resistance...?

—Excerpt from "Why is it so easy to muster
up strength and energy for unimportant tasks...?"
e-zine article—www.alduncan.net

People get jammed up because while looking for the path of least resistance, if they aren't careful they end up on the path of most resistance.

Duncan Nugget #235
There is nothing wrong with looking for a smarter way to do something, but don't get "smart" and "easy" confused. They are not always the same thing. A little resistance in the beginning is better than facing a lot of unnecessary resistance in the end.

Million-Dollar Question:
What are you doing that has you seeking the path of least resistance and is it REALLY the path of least resistance in the long run?

GUARANTEED ENERGY WASTERS

I once heard someone complaining about not having enough water pressure in her house. When the plumber she hired came to look at the problem he found out that she had a leaky pipe.

There was nothing technically wrong with the water pressure. The plumber fixed the leak and her water pressure was fine. It works the same way with energy. (And money!)

Duncan Nugget #236
It isn't always about needing more energy; sometimes it's about wasting less energy.

Million-Dollar Question:
What are you wasting your energy on?

Did TV pop into your head? Maybe negative people also came to mind. Well, regardless of what came to mind, here are nine guaranteed energy wasters that you want to avoid:

9 Guaranteed Energy Wasters and A Few Words About Them

1. Worrying—Getting worked up over petty things.

According to *The Fog of Worry* (Earl Nightingale) 92% of the things we worry about never happen. That is bonkers. This also includes worrying about things you have no control over and *"analysis-paralysis"* (over-analyzing things).

2. Watching TV, especially late night TV.

Have you ever been trying to watch TV, but the TV is really watching you?!

If you are struggling to watch something and you keep falling asleep every 2 minutes then go to bed. Seriously—it's hard to balance a remote in one hand, your glass or cup in your other hand, and keep your head from bobbing all over the place as you try to figure out what you just missed while you were "resting your eyes".

3. Traffic—Sitting in the car, getting stressed out, and hollering at somebody that can't even hear you!

I am definitely guilty of this one. Sometimes I wish I was Mr.

Fantastic from the Fantastic Four so that I could just stretch my elastic arm out of the window over to the other car and smack that idiot driver right upside his head! (I know. That's terrible, right?) This is really just another case of getting worked up over petty things.

4. Hanging around Wraith

There was a TV show called *Stargate Atlantis* that used to come on the SyFy Channel. On this show there were a group of aliens called the Wraith. Guess what the main source of food is for the Wraith. Humans.

But the Wraith don't feed on human blood or flesh, these aliens feed on humans by sucking all of the energy out of them. Whenever the Wraith finished feeding, the victim looked a 190-year old raisin. That's the same effect negative people have on you. They literally drain your energy. As soon as they walk in the room or start talking to you, you can feel it. They can take any good idea and make it bad. They can take any good day and make it sad. Psychologists have proven that emotions and attitudes are contagious. Stay away from Wraith!

5. Fruitless Fantasizing

There's a BIG difference between visualization and fantasizing. When you've got your mind completely focused on your goals and dreams and when you're thinking vivid, successful thoughts,

it's called visualizing your victory. On the other hand, if you find yourself daydreaming and thinking things like:

"Man, I don't how that guy won $130 million dollars! If I won that kind of money I would buy me a..."

Or you could be thinking things like: *"Girl, if I ever had a chance to go out with Ne-Yo..."* (or Zac Effron, Leonardo Dicaprio, Denzel, George Clooney or anybody you think is ridiculously hot). That's called fruitless fantasizing.

You might be thinking, *"Al, fantasizing about Rihanna is not fruitless!"*

Listen, spending all of your time fantasizing about things you don't really plan on doing or things that are unlikely to happen is a serious waste of mental energy.

6. The Snack Attack—Eating Too Much Junk Food

This is another one I struggle with. I gotta have my snacks!

Imagine this:

Too busy to cook...working on your dreams...concentrating on school or work....a ton of activities to do or maybe you have to deal with your kids or younger brothers and sisters and of course, the list goes on. There is no way you have time to get something proper to eat, right? Instead, it's fast food time or pretzels, cookies, chips, dip, candy, and candy bar time.

A little while later, after you eat all of this junk, you can't figure out why you're dead tired. It's the salt, sugar, and all of the stuff on the label that you can't pronounce. All of that is messing with you blood-sugar levels and draining your energy.

Once this happens people start to break out the heavy hitters like Starbucks, Mountain Dew, and Red Bull. It'll really give you wings, but it won't help you land. A few hours later you come crashing down to Earth and you end up feeling like crap, so you have to do it all over again. Unfortunately, some people—especially some college students—get hooked on the prescription drug adderall. **NOT COOL.**

I don't care how or why you justify this behavior; in the long run it's bad for your health.

My rule is: if it is something that requires all of my brain power then no junk food allowed until it's done.

(NOTE: I have to admit that this rule is HARD for me to follow and at times, I break it. When I do, I pay the price. My craving might be satisfied, but my energy and alertness suffer.)

If it's something that I'm doing while I'm chillaxin', like watching a game or a movie, then junk food (in moderation) isn't too bad. It's still not great, but I already told you that I struggle with this one.

7. Stress

You probably already know that being stressed out kills your energy, but did you know that **over 70% of all doctor visits are stress related?** Here are a few easy stress busters.

- ✓ **Exercise**—Not only will it decrease your stress, it will give you a lot more energy.
- ✓ **Get Organized**—Being organized will cut down on some of the unnecessary stress of rushing around and feeling unprepared.
- ✓ **Delegate**—If you are a leader or an entrepreneur, trying to do everything yourself is a guaranteed way to stress yourself out. When possible, turn the "M" upside down. Take it from "me" to "we". This includes knowing when to say "No".
- ✓ **Stay out of other people's drama.** Take inventory of the people in your life and if you can't bring them up, don't let them bring you down.
- ✓ **Crying—in moderation.** Yes...even for tough guys, a good healthy cry can be helpful. Stress producing chemicals are removed from your body via your tears, but too much crying is not cool. It might even be a sign of depression.
- ✓ **Laughter**—Humor is one the most effective ways to relieve stress. Find the humor in a situation. Watch a funny movie or check out your favorite comedian. Or just find some stupid people to laugh at. There are always plenty of them around. (Hey, I know that's po-

litically incorrect, but it's not my fault they're idiots!)

✓ **Eat healthier**—Not only will junk food drain your energy, it can also increase your stress.

✓ **Get enough sleep**—Constantly working while you're sleep deprived will add to your stress.

✓ **Take breaks**—take breaks at regular intervals (once every 30-60 minutes is good). Stretch, get some air, go for a walk, or do all three.

✓ **Avoid Self-Medication a.k.a Gettin' High or Drunk**—Drugs and Alcohol may seem like relief, but they cover up the problems, not solve the problems.

✓ **Share or get help**—Talk about it with a good friend, a relative, or get some help. There are a ton of free resources for dealing with stress. You can find a lot of them on the internet.

8. Improper Breathing

When you constantly take short, shallow breaths (only breathing from your chest) you are robbing yourself of oxygen. Practice taking at least 5-10 deep breaths (from your lower abdomen) an hour and watch how your energy and alertness increases.

9. The #1 Cause of Daytime Fatigue

Do you know the #1 cause of daytime fatigue?

The answer is a lot more basic than most people realize. According to research, **it's the lack of water.**

Your brain uses a tremendous amount of energy. (I'm not sure if that's true for everybody!) It needs to be consistently re-hydrated. A small level of dehydration makes it difficult for you to maintain concentration and produces sluggishness with

dull headaches. The brain is 75% water and needs to be well hydrated to work efficiently. If you've been feeling drained and tired during the day, increase your water intake. The results may surprise you.

I work better under pressure.

Garbage.

That statement is the master procrastinator's most powerful—or should I say weakest—excuse. I hear it from people all the time and I love it because then I get to respond with:

"Oh yeah? Well, why don't you put some pressure on yourself to do what you need to do and get where you need to be in more timely fashion?"

The look on their faces: priceless.

Pressure can be the result of procrastination or the moment. Successfully dealing with the pressure of an important moment will help you grow. It will elevate you to a new plateau and strengthen your self-confidence.

Pressure that results from procrastination, however, perpetuates your disrespect for time and keeps you in a rut.

This type of pressure is an excuse for your inability to focus on the task at hand. People try to use "the last minute" as a tool for focusing because they have yet to develop the willpower to focus on their own.

Think about that.

—Excerpt from A State of Mind Called Time Pt. III
e-zine article—www.alduncan.net

5 Fatigue Fighters and A Few Words About Them

1. Power Nap (or Break)

I touched on this when we talked about stress busters. A 15-20 minute nap during the day will do you wonders. Take two and you will feel brand new. If you can't realistically take a power nap then at least take breaks at regular intervals.

While taking your break—CHILLAX. Don't do your bills or get organized. You might even want to avoid making phone calls. Chillax means "chill and relax", not "work less".

2. A Good Night's Sleep

This has got to be one of the hardest things to come by nowadays. People do not get enough sleep, especially teenagers.

According to U.S. News and Special Reports teenagers need more sleep than any other age group, including newborns and toddlers! Ironically, because of school, work, and activities, teens usually get the least amount of sleep. So, when teens are sleeping most of the weekend away, they aren't necessarily being lazy. I know that's hard to believe, but it's a fact.

The proper amount of sleep is relative. For years, I've been doing very well with 4-5 hours of sleep per night, but keep in mind that I take at least two Power Naps during the day.

How much sleep should you get?

"Sleep is a behavior and, like all behaviors, it varies greatly among people...The greatest differences occur in the timing of sleep and the amount of sleep—the factors which are most important in determining whether you will wake up feeling

rested...Many people don't pay attention to the timing of their sleep...Yet delaying or altering the time you go to sleep can have a major impact on how you feel when you wake up."

Dr. Carol Landis
Sleep researcher and associate professor
Biobehavioral Nursing and Health Systems

People sleep better at different times during their daily cycle. While some people function better if they go to sleep early and rise early, others may feel more rested and alert when they stay up late and sleep in.

The amount of sleep the average adult needs each night also varies. Some people may be fine with six hours sleep, while others need up to nine hours per night. Dr. Landis explains that those who follow a regular sleep schedule are more likely to function better on fewer hours. She also says that most adults need at least six hours of sleep each night.

(NOTE: Once you sleep past your ideal amount of time you will probably wake up tired.)

3. Eating Water-Rich Foods

"Be a good boy, Jimmy. Eat your vegetables."

Eating foods that have a high concentration of water helps to keep your brain hydrated. These types of food also require less energy to digest. (Your digestive system uses up to one third of your energy. That's why you get so tired after a big meal.)

Here are some examples of water-rich foods:

✓ Broccoli
✓ Cabbage
✓ Cauliflower
✓ Cucumbers

✓ Grapes
✓ Grapefruit
✓ Lettuce
✓ Oranges

✓ Pasta dishes with extra vegetables

✓ Radishes

✓ Smoothies

✓ Soup

✓ Spinach

✓ Tomatoes

✓ Watermelon

4. Do What You Love to Do

That's what this book is all about.

It doesn't matter if you have a crazy work schedule, a busy family life, or even if you are in school, you want to make time to do what you love to do.

Even it's only for a short amount of time everyday or once or twice a month. Doing the things you love to do in life is not only fulfilling, it's stimulating. Your happiness will increase, you'll love life a whole lot more, and you'll have more energy. You'll be fired up.

Hopefully, what you love to do isn't something that is damaging to your mind and body or the well-being of others. If that's the case then you need to find something else to love...immediately.

5. Instant Energy Triggers

There are certain things that will give you a burst of energy. It could be your favorite song that gets you hyped up, a special person in your life, or a certain type of motion like clapping your hands or jumping up and down. These are called triggers or anchors. Everybody has them, but everyone isn't aware of them.

You can set up your own triggers by doing the exercise that I had you do at the beginning of this chapter.

a. Think of a time when you were excited and fired up. On a scale of 1 to 10, make it a 10.

b. Now turn it up to a 12. Hold it there and enjoy the feeling.

c. Now turn it up to a 15. Hold it there and enjoy the feeling.

d. Now do something to anchor the feeling. You could clap your hands, slap your leg, touch you arm, yell "Boom!" or whatever you want to do.

e. Do this entire exercise several times and then go start working on whatever you need to do. This exercise will give you a nice burst of energy. If you've avoided the Energy Wasters and used, the other Fatigue Fighters we've talked about the energy burst will last longer.

NOTHING HAPPENS WITHOUT ENERGY

You can have all the goals and dreams in the world. You can have outstanding plans and ideas to make them happen, but none of that will do you any good without the physical, emotional, and mental energy to carry things out. You must refuse to allow anything or anyone (including YOU) to waste your energy.

Duncan Nugget #237
Your energy is the most
precious resource you have.
Guard it like your life depends
on it because...it does.

LIVE YOUR DREAMS

Kevin Hogan, Psy.D.

 Kevin Hogan holds a doctorate in Psychology and is the author of eleven books (and counting...). He is a Body Language Expert and Unconscious Influence Expert to the BBC, the *New York Post* and dozens of popular magazines like *InTouch*, *First for Women*, *Success!*, and *Cosmopolitan*. He has become the go-to resource for analyzing key White House figures. Hogan has taught Persuasion and Influence at the University of St. Thomas Management Center and is a frequent media guest. Articles by and about him have appeared in *Success!*, *Redbook*, *Office Pro*, *Selling Power*, *Cosmopolitan*, *Maxim*, *Playboy* and numerous other publications. He was recently featured in a half dozen magazines (including *wProst*) in Poland after teaching persuasion and influence skills to that country's 350 leading sales managers.

Kevin Hogan is generally agreed to be the nation's leading body language expert. Kevin is a dynamic, well-known international public speaker, consultant and corporate trainer. He has trained persuasion, sales and marketing skills to leaders in the government of Poland, employees from Boeing, Microsoft, Starbucks, Cargill, Pillsbury, Carlson Companies, Fortis Insurance, Great Clips, the State of Minnesota, 3M, The United States Postal Service and numerous other Fortune 500 companies. He recently spoke to The Inner Circle and at the Million Dollar Roundtable (MDRT) convention in Las Vegas.

His keynotes, seminars and workshops help companies sell, market and communicate more effectively. His cutting edge research into the mind and keen understanding of consumer behavior create a unique distillation of information never before released to the public. Each customized program he leads is fit specifically to the needs of the group or organization. Kevin will give your people new and easy to implement ideas to achieve excellence.

To make Kevin Hogan the dynamic speaker (read that as very dynamic, funny, informative and knock 'em dead!) for your next event, e-mail kevin@kevinhogan.com with your event details and get a personal response.

Books by Kevin Hogan include:
- ✓ The Psychology of Persuasion: How to Persuade Others to Your Way of Thinking
- ✓ The Science of Influence
- ✓ Selling: Powerful New Strategies for Sales Success
- ✓ Covert Persuasion

V

The Psychology of Living Your Dreams: Inside the Mind of Kevin Hogan, Psy.D

Body Language Expert, Unconscious Influence Expert, Author

"You can't change how you were born, but you can change your decisions along the way."
– Kevin Hogan

From a young boy in with a degree in poverty to an international best-selling author with a doctorate's degree in Psychology, the journey of Kevin Hogan has been remarkable.

Born in one of the poorest sections of Chicago, Illinois and raised in a single parent home, Dr. Hogan is the oldest of five siblings. *"It was my job to be dad to four kids."* With that kind of start in life, few people, if any, would have predicted that he would reach such a high level of achievement. Nonetheless, equipped with unwavering work-ethic and dogged determination, Dr. Hogan has overcome low expectations, conquered the poverty mindset, and is living the life of his dreams.

HUMBLE BEGINNINGS

Al Duncan: Both of us come from humble beginnings...

Kevin Hogan: Boy, that's a nice way to say it!

Yeah, I guess that is a nice way to say it—the polite way to say "ghetto"! How were you able to overcome low expectations, the negative environment, and the poverty mindset? How did you get past those things?

I believe that I was lucky in one way that you [Al Duncan] weren't. When I was a kid, my family had a similar amount of money as yours, but our neighborhood was basically crime free. Well, there was always something going on, but we didn't have the major stuff—people weren't killing each other.

They definitely were in my neighborhood.

We were more mischievous than really wicked and I think that might have made a piece of the difference for me. When you have that violence I think it's challenging to overcome that. Which is why, among other reasons, I have a great deal of respect for you, Al.

But on the money end we have the person who made $500,000 this year, the person who made $1,000,000 this year, and the person who made $30,000 this year and the thing is, everybody worked hard. We are exhausted, stressed out, beat up, and everybody's tired. So, what's the difference?

The difference really is that the people who succeed refuse to fail permanently anymore. When you look back to how you grew up you have to look back and say, "I'm not going to do that anymore. I'm not going to be there any more. I'm not going to tolerate that life anymore."

**"The difference really is that
the people who succeed refuse to
fail permanently anymore."**

FAIL, FAIL, FAIL, AND THEN FAIL AGAIN

You can't change how you were born, but you can change your decisions along the way. And I think that little propulsion system away from the pain of poverty, severe lower income, or whatever you want to call it, if you think about it, it's huge. When you understand that the more decisions you're making the more often you are failing and succeeding then you'll understand that it's okay to fail 10, 20, 50, or 100 times. The people who are successful are the people who say, "Failing is so terrible that I don't want to deal with that anymore, but I don't mind failing 50 times if I get ten successes."

PERFECTION IS THE PROBLEM

How can a person be okay with failing when failing can feel so humiliating?

Part of it is that I had to get past having to get it perfect. People who have done pretty well in life realize that they want to do a great job for people. They want to be as good as they possibly can, but they don't try to be perfect anymore.

We tried to be perfect when we were young. We would get an A- or a B+ instead of an A+ and the thing is how much more could we have learned if a B+ would've been okay? What else could we have handled? Did we really need to get the A+? So, perfection is a big one. Knock that out and refuse to go through that anymore.

Be willing to say, "You know what? I did this event wrong or I was terrible or my book failed and that's okay." If people can be okay with failure and be willing to say that it's okay to fail 50 times this year to get those ten successes then I think they're going to win.

It's like I used to tell Katie when we first got married—I don't think she ever believed me—but I told her we're going to fire off a lot of rockets in our life and some of them are going to make it to the moon. Most of them won't. And sure 'nuff that's the deal. Some made it, most didn't, but one of them did so well it might have made it to Mars! So, I want to see people fail with the intent of continuing on, having some successes, and when they screw up letting it be okay.

IT WAS THE WORST OF TIMES

Of course, a lot of people think that they have more or worse problems than everybody else. So, while we're on this topic, give me a snapshot of what you're neighborhood was like and some of the challenges you faced.

We were living very, very poor. I'll never forget the Thanksgiving of '73 when the Boy Scouts came with all the bags of food. My brother and I knew that they would be bringing clothes, too and we didn't want to be there because we hated getting all of that plaid. We hated the idea of having to wear "not cool" clothes to school. However, having "not cool" clothes was superseded by the choice of not having any clothes. Things were tight. My mom had no money, my Dad left for California and left us behind. We couldn't have had less money, but we could've had a less livable environment. We could've had major criminals and shooting and all of that. None of that existed.

"Having 'not cool' clothes was superseded by the choice of not having any clothes."

SELLING YOUR WAY OUT

What were you doing right before you started speaking professionally and how did you make the transition?

I was selling advertising for a Veteran's Incentive Project in Minneapolis, Minnesota. The Vietnam Veterans came back like our men and women do from Iraq. They come back and nobody's there. In WWII there was a parade when they came back. Everybody was proud. But coming back from Vietnam and Iraq nobody was really proud. They didn't get the parade and they should. They lived through hell. Over 10-14 years a lot of them develop mental illnesses, which is what's happening to our guys in Iraq. So, a large percentage of them became homeless, disproportionate to the population. It seemed like out of every three homeless people on the streets of Minneapolis one of them was a Vietnam Vet. It was that pronounced back in 1984 or 1985.

One day I ran into a Vietnam vet named John Fields. John was trying to build a way that Vietnam vets who were homeless could become productive again in society. And they started a program called the Veteran's Incentive Project. The guys were VIP's. This wasn't a VIP place. It was like I grew up. Very impoverished, but it was a cool concept. John got a grant from a non-profit organization called the McKnight Foundation and he hired me to be their fundraising/sales director. He wanted me to go out and raise money for the organization. He also wanted me to teach guys how to write resumes and how to present themselves better and how to communicate with people.

The first check I got cleared, the second one didn't, and the third one didn't. But the thing is that he was trying hard, but the only thing we had was the $5000 from the grant. So, I started selling advertising on the back of discount cards to raise money for the organization and to pay my salary. That was somewhat successful for a couple of years until the organization didn't receive its money from the United Way.

IMPACTING THE YOUTH

When the organization folded I had to do something. I couldn't stand the idea of working in an office that was in the dark because I couldn't turn the lights on. So, I went out and I started a non-profit organization with seven other people called Success Dynamics for Children. The organization actually grew for maybe 5 or 6 years. We did okay and we helped a lot of kids get off drugs and stay off drugs. We produced a good drug prevention message and I was real proud that we were able to make a little inroad. We even got some recognition.

I'll never forget the day when the mail man comes to the door and says, "Wow! You must 'rate'."

"Why?", I asked.

"Because you have a letter here from the White House."

I'm thinking, "Shoot! The IRS must've nailed me!" My heart started pounding and then I realized, "Oh. It's the White House, not Ogden, Utah."

It was a two or three line letter from the President saying congratulations on the good work you're doing. That sort of gave me momentum to say, "You know what I want to keep doing this." So, I started out speaking in front of little kids—kindergarten to fourth grade, all the different young kids. And you know what? Some of those audiences were tough!

Yeah, you started with the hardest audiences first!

KIDS—YA GOTTA LOVE'EM

I confess. I love little kids because I'm kind of a little kid my-self. It was tough, but I really liked talking to the kids. I thought it was cool. I would get down on my knees, eye-level with them and I got a good message across. I helped them to find ways that they could be better at a being themselves.

Drugs are such a big problem in America. I remember a little girl came up to me and said, "Kevin, my mom and dad are using cocaine and they're not very nice when they do it." And she went on to describe a bunch of stuff that was going on at her house. She just wanted a hug. Little stuff like that is why I loved doing it.

I've never been a great speaker. I've always been just a work-ing kind of guy, you know? But I related well with what kids were going through and it was nice to make some impact when I had a chance to be in front of those kids.

THE TRUTH ABOUT PASSION

I believe that you have to do what you love; you have to pursue your passion. But when is passion not enough?

That is the perfect question because ultimately you want to end up doing what you love. If you love playing the guitar, you want to ultimately end up playing the guitar. In fact, I just got done playing the guitar before we talked and you should consider yourself lucky that you didn't have to hear it! I've been playing this thing for ten years and it's still dissonant!

So, my passion was to play guitar, right? But I wasn't silly enough to think that McCartney [of the singing group the Bea-tles] was going to hire me on after he left George and Ringo [members of the Beatles]. I knew that I was going to have to do one of my passions without getting paid for it.

Writing was also a passion of mine. I always loved journalism and writing stories. I wanted to be some kind of writer when I grew up. I wasn't a good writer, just an average writer, but I wanted to write. I will tell you that when you first start out you are not going to be able to pay the bills just because you write a book.

Man, isn't that the truth?!

In fact, it could take you 4 ½ years just to get an acceptance letter from a publisher. I'm not sure of the exact number, but it was about 247 submissions and rejections before Pelican Publishing in Louisiana said yes to my book, *The Psychology of Persuasion*. We call that either stupid or persistence! Those were the same people who published Zig Ziglar's *See You at the Top*. My book was pretty good and I was proud of it, but I couldn't live off the money I made on that back in '96-'98.

So, while you are doing your passion, which is cool, you have to be willing to do anything else while you are working on getting to those things that you love to do.

THE MISSING ATTITUDE

When my first step-dad died back in 1975, on the road before that, prior to his death, we knew he had congestive heart failure so, we knew he was going to die. My real dad had just left in 1966 so, there were about four bad years when my step-dad was in the hospital and times were not so acceptable.

And in those days I'd go from door to door. I'd say, "Hey can I pull your weeds for a dollar? Or "Can I shovel your snow for $3." I did any thing it took to produce something for the house—anything. That's really the attitude that's necessary and it's missing in our world a lot. People will say "You're just a rich guy." And I say, "Uh-uh. I'm a poor guy in a big house." And then they'll say "I'm unemployed." And I'm thinking they can walk, they can talk, and they can breathe. Unless they're on life support, I want to see that person working.

Right! I totally agree. At the very least he or she should aggressively be looking for employment or trying to start a business.

I have empathy for the situation because I've experienced it. I know exactly what it's like to be going through a very tough time. But I have no sympathy for somebody who isn't willing to go out there and bust their butt for their family. And I think that when people get to the point where it's like personal pride comes in and you say to yourself, "You know what this is my family, man."

"You have to be willing to do anything else while you are working on getting to those things that you love to do."

THE JANITOR: WILLING AND ABLE

For my first two years of college I was at the Cannon Falls Nursing Home in Minnesota because I had to do something. I didn't get a scholarship; I got a $196 Pell grant from the government.

So, passion is really important, but when you have to pull the weeds or spray the neighbor's yard with pesticide or mow the lawns, do it. People have to do whatever it takes until they can go do their passion or until they can find a job that's cooler than whatever they're doing right now. People who are willing to do that are going to succeed.

If you are willing to care enough about your family, about your personal self, and about your self-worth then you won't just let somebody [the government] cut you a check for long. You will get your butt out there. You will go do something. You will make a difference even if it's being a janitor. That's one of the reasons I start my CD's off saying, "This is Kevin Hogan—your author, your narrator, your janitor." I was the janitor.

People have got to be willing to do anything to get to their passion because if you're only willing to do what you're qualified for, what if that job gets shipped over seas? You've got to be constantly evolving, constantly doing things that are going to pay the bills. Keep in the habit of being productive and valuable to your family.

BUST YOUR BUTT

Everything that you've been talking about requires a lot of stamina and resolve. How can someone develop the stamina and resolve to make their dreams come to fruition?

This is where personal pride begins. It's so important that people think in terms of their families as opposed to what somebody owes them or how the world is evil. There's a lot of tough stuff going on out there. One-hundred thousand people died in Burma and we couldn't even get food to the survivors because the place is run by these crazy dictators. So, there's a lot of bad stuff going on in the world and people have just got to say, "You know what? I've got a family. I'm 18, 22, 24, or whatever and I want my family to be proud of me. So, I'm going to go out there and bust my butt so, that my mom or whoever's helping me out can be proud of me."

You went out and you tried. That's the whole deal right there. Did you sit there and do nothing or did you try? My mom used to say, "If you don't work, you don't eat." And that was really true. That was real and it was a metaphor for everything.

As soon as you have a wife and/or a kid or a husband, as soon as you have somebody who depends on you, you can't sit and take a day off from work. If you lose a job then you go to Target the same day and get a job pushing carts or start your own lawn service business or something and never let the world see you acting too good to do anything. I've done every menial job on this planet that I can think of. Well, maybe not the circus one.

"Did you sit there and do nothing or did you try?"

MAKE YOUR MOM PROUD

You want people to be proud of you and you want to be proud of yourself. You can't be proud of yourself if the only thing you're willing to do is the job that you're trained to do. You are expected to do the job you've been trained to do. What makes you special and what makes you a great person is caring enough about your family to do every job when you have an opportunity. If you can walk and breathe, you should be doing something to make your family better. There's personal pride there.

If it takes more than that to get a person motivated then you have got to look at your mother one more time. That lady gave birth to you. She was there and dad might not have been. So, people need to bust their butts because moms need to look at their kids and say, "You know what? I'm proud of my kid because he worked really hard." Moms are under-appreciated people.

People say stuff like, "Oh I got laid off. I ain't gonna work." Screw that. What would your mom say? She would want to see you doing something that would make her proud. And people need to think of that. That's powerful motivation right there.

I know God is looking down at you, but he sends mom to beat you across the butt if you're doing something wrong! Your mom should be able to tell a story about you to someone else saying how proud she is of you. Give her something good to talk about even though times are tough in Philadelphia or Chicago or where ever. If she can tell a story about you then her life has even more meaning.

THE ULTIMATE NIGHTMARE

What's the most challenging thing about being a professional speaker?

There are a lot of things, but the first thing that comes to my mind was when I was in Milwaukee two years ago when everything went wrong. It's the ultimate nightmare when you're the focal point of attention and you're jokes don't work, you don't tell your stories well, everything goes to heck in a hand basket. You've just had a bad day. It's like striking out at the plate like fives times in a row and you're thinking, "Please take the blinders off of my eyes. I know I can hit this ball." That's the hardest thing. When you fail in front of 150 people and you realize that you're just like everybody else.

REGRETS? NOT OVER HERE

You've had a challenging life, but you've also lived a very full life and you've done a lot of great things. If there were one thing in your life you could've done differently, what would it be?

You know, Al, there's not a lot I would've done differently. I've got to be honest. Maybe little tiny things here and there along the way—I made mistakes. But overall I think I did the things I needed to do at the time and don't regret them. So, I wouldn't change anything that I had control of, honest to God. Maybe, I could've been easier to deal with for my wife because, you know, they're moms, too. But of all the major life decisions along the way, I don't believe I would change anything. I don't think there's anything that I would've done differently.

EYE ON THE FUTURE

I know that you like short term goals best, but where will Kevin Hogan be in five years?

My daughter starts the University of Minnesota this year and in five years my son will be fifteen which means I'll still be important in his life, but not necessary! At that point he'll have a girlfriend and I'll probably go back to doing more cool events around the world. I've spent the past few years more at home most of the time so that I could be with my kids. That's important to me. But as things change, I'll probably do more events.

DOING YOUR PASSION IS SPECIAL

I understand how McCartney, Elvis, Elton John, and those types of people feel. When you get up in front of that audience and you are doing your passion and you don't screw up and you're doing okay, those days really are special. So, whatever your passion is, you do want to get there and do that and do it often enough to be relevant to you.

"People have got to be willing to do anything to get to their passion."

VI.
The Goal-Setting System That Works

By Kevin Hogan, Psy.D
(Excerpt from "Manifesting the Millionaire Mind")

"A goal is a dream with a deadline."

Nonsense!

It doesn't really work that way...and once people figure that out, they sometimes become disenchanted, frustrated, feel a sense of failure, and worse, they feel inadequate. And there is no reason for any of this.

There are a lot of myths about goal setting.

There are a lot of goals that need to be set.

How do you know what kinds of goals to set and what will actually be the most constructive system to achieve those goals? I'm going to show you.

A dream with a deadline is most likely to remain a dream.

It is almost a guaranteed recipe for failure.

Goal setting as it is typically taught rarely works. There is, however, a system that is actually likely to succeed with predictability. Before we get to the opening stages of the system...a couple of thumbnail sketches of success...

The Beatles didn't sit down and plan on being the most successful rock group in history. Elvis didn't set a goal to become the number one performer in the history of the world.

**A dream with a deadline is most likely
to remain a dream.**

Achievement seems to work a bit differently than starting with a goal. In fact, success doesn't start with setting a goal. Elvis loved to sing. He cut a record for his Mom as a birthday present and the studio owner couldn't believe how good it was. Elvis always had just loved to sing—gospel, blues, and country. He did some local events and had a great time. His dream, his goal was to get on the Grand Ole Opry. They told him to go back to driving a truck. He had no chance of success.

The negative reaction in Nashville hurt the young Presley and motivated him and his backup band to get more gigs, learn more songs, and have more fun...and they did. A set of movie contracts tied the young man up for a period of 8 years at which time he once again went back to what he loved—singing to a live audience. It was then that he realized his dream. It wasn't to be #1, it was to have fun. While he was on track and having fun he succeeded richly. When he was off track, his life self-destructed.

> ## "A winner is someone who recognizes his God-given talents, works his tail off to develop them into skills, and uses those skills to accomplish his goals."
>
> —Larry Bird, Hall of Fame basketball player

The Beatles story was similar. From '60-'62, they just wanted to have fun, keep getting better, write songs, and live a dream. They never planned on becoming #1. All of them were often quoted as saying that they would be lucky to see their success continue another few months. Like Elvis, their goals were largely short-term. Learn more songs, get better as musicians, put out as much good material as they could. And...have fun. While they were having fun they succeeded. Once other things became more important than the current dream of playing, they bitterly split. The residual from their work never dwindled and they all succeeded in their new careers as soloists, as we know.

When you analyze those who succeed at anything, they do so doing something they are either a) good at or b) love or c) both.

When you look at the lives of people who live unfulfilled lives, they often have as much skill as those who love their work, but they are not doing what they love.

The foundation of goal setting is laid in the love of the dream. Is the dream a nightmare, or is it truly a dream? Many people are very skilled, say, as a musician only because their parents made them play when they were children, but they don't actually enjoy their playing to any significant degree.

Where there is no desire, there is no passion for the goal.

It's very hard to artificially generate a passion for something you don't love. That doesn't mean you can't enjoy success at it, however. Someone who has a passion for financial independence and the lifestyle it brings, can definitely do something they don't enjoy to achieve that goal.

Clearly a life where one lives a life that one enjoys and one where you are doing what you love is superior to any other alternative, so as you think of mid-term and long-term goals, you want to think in terms of doing something that rewards you just for doing it. Something you might do for the love of the experience itself.

This is more than just a useful philosophy. This is good neuroscience.

Desire drives emotion. Emotion is fundamental to attention. Attention is necessary for acquisition.

In other words: If you have to try and think about your goal and actually might forget about it from day to day or hour to hour, the goal could be worthwhile, but it is very unlikely to ever manifest in reality. The vast majority of your brain function operates out of your awareness. Whatever the emotional and survival elements of the brain focus on (outside of your awareness) are what you are likely to be driven to move toward and away from. Your brain will focus on what will fulfill your desires and bring you into a desirable state of being. (This state differs from person to person. Some people need calm. Others excitement. There is no universal state of being that is desirable for everyone, though everyone does seem to benefit from the ability to be calm at least some of the time.)

If you think it would be desirable to become a manager at your company, but you are emotionally being driven away from your work to find fulfillment elsewhere, your goal-setting is going to most likely to be met with a lot of frustration. Even if you are successful.

There are a number of aspects of life in which you can achieve goals. There are a number of careers, jobs, lifestyles you can live with and even thrive on. The first area of true consideration is: what are some of those possibilities?

The first principle I want you to carve into your tablet of stone is:

You are far more likely to achieve any goal if you are truly attached to it in some emotional way.

Does it bring out feelings of excitement, calm, passion, love, joy, intensity?

Emotions do affect your decision-making process. When you are going through a period of negative emotions, you need to work through those emotions until you come to place of stability. You may have heard the phrase, "All feelings are okay." I disagree.

The Dalai Lama explored this concept in the book, Destructive Emotions, edited by Daniel Goleman. The conclusion was that there are destructive emotions, which affect you in every way. Do not become a slave to your destructive emotions. Do not set goals when you are in the grips of destructive emotions. FARG-ing feelings are destructive, not constructive (Fear, Anger, Resentment, Guilt). It is important to be aware of your feelings and take them into account, knowing these feelings are a filter for your environment. Don't let your negative emotions distort your goal setting process.

The second principle I want you to write in your tablet of stone is that where your attention is largely determines what your outcome will actually be. Here is a certainty:

Where you put your attention is where you are likely to go.

If you focus on what you don't want, you may very well find yourself getting it anyway. There is nothing metaphysical about this. Again, it's simple science. Whatever pictures you put in your brain are the only pieces of information your brain can utilize to direct the body toward or away from. If your response to your fear is phobic, your brain will do everything in it's power to move you away from the stimulus. In these cases, say the fear of extreme poverty can and will absolutely cause you to work hard to avoid poverty. A phobia and powerful fear can definitely move you away from something.

However, when you are thinking of choices that are neither phobic nor are you passionate about them, you have a very different situation. Your brain will lock onto these images and move you toward them. If there are many different pictures that don't have a common theme, you will simply move in multiple directions. This may not be a bad thing. If your goals are to be "a little of everything" then that is very legitimate and could be very fulfilling. Most people however, have a sense of dream or purpose. My job is to show you specifically how to set goals so you get there!

The third principle is that although long term goals are very useful, I am far more concerned about your short and mid term goals.

Put the majority of your attention on the goals that are going to come to fruition (or not!) soon.

Therefore: Set short-term goals that you can use to evaluate how your journey is going. (Ex. Are you having fun? Are you learning what you need to learn? Are you seeing how your current activity is directly related to your longer-term success?)

Long-term goals are typically not compelling for most people. Everyone knows they should save $10,000 per year from now until retirement so they can retire with security, but less than 1% will actually do what they need to. They will instead do what they want. Assume that you will do this as well (at least for now!)

Deadlines are another story.

A story...

Six years ago, I wanted to start a school. Having met some of my life goals (write 10 books, speak internationally, be a good Dad, etc.) I wanted to establish the first licensed school for hypnosis in Minnesota. I had a clear vision of what I wanted to do. I had determined very specific outcomes.

Curriculum, location, standards...and a date. I put it out one year. For me that is a long time-horizon on projects like this. I'm used to moving at lightning speed...

Everything was done at the 4-month mark except licensure. Licensure was to be my last project because I've never been one to enjoy paperwork, deal in the minutia of governmental bureaucracy and well...you get the idea. Surely we could accomplish the paperwork and pay the exorbitant fees for licensure in a matter of weeks.

Not a chance.

Oh, the money was all paid up front. The State doesn't accept applications without big checks attached. It was then one year until the state would issue the license. Total time: 16 months.

The problem with deadlines is that most people come to a deadline, pass it then quit. "It just wasn't meant to be"...one tends to whisper. There is more to a goal than having a dream with a deadline.

Having a plan, a schedule, and a clear picture of the outcome are all critical to success.

Then there are other elements including *contingency plans* and *persisting in the face of adversity*, among others. Don't lock yourself into an all or nothing date by which you MUST achieve something.

Get ready in the next part to start to apply the principles of goal setting. Enjoy the exercises that will be presented. Take your time and enjoy this process. If it's not fun, then you are thinking about someone else's life! This should be a RICH experience!

Conclusion:

We learned the first 3 Applied Principles of Effective Goal Setting.

1. You are far more likely to achieve any goal if you are truly attached to it in some emotional way.

2. Where your attention is (good or bad, positive or negative) largely determines what your outcome will actually be.

3. Put the majority of your attention on the goals that are going to come to fruition (or not!) soon. (Shorter-term goals are more effective.)

Alix Graham-Michel — Aligram Designs

With a love for sewing instilled by her mother and grandmother, Alix began working with needle and thread at a very early age. Following a career with the United Nations in New York, she decided to follow her own "pattern" or passion in life. She left the UN offices to run a home-based custom clothing, interior decorating and design business. In order to build her natural flair and skill, Alix attended FIT and also earned a certificate in Fashion Design, Patternmaking, and Clothing Construction from the French Fashion Academy.

Her work has been seen on the international film screen, worn by musical performers and auctioned at national benefits. Alix's work has also been widely published in the leading sewing magazines. Second only to her three children, her love for sewing knows few bounds. Today, Alix is a TV personality and an international educator teaching in the United States, Canada and South America. She loves to teach and help others find their passion for sewing.

Popular Programs by Alix:

- ✓ Passion for Sewing™
- ✓ Luxurious Peignoir
- ✓ Spring Fling Table Runner
- ✓ 3-D Butterfly Table Runner
- ✓ Pretty in PJ's
- ✓ Specialty Techniques
- ✓ Elegant Boudoir Pillow
- ✓ Sensational Serger Jacket
- ✓ Patterning Fitting & Tailoring

Office: 305.433.4088

Fax: 302.338.4088

www.aligram.com

alix@aligram.com

VII.
A Passion for Sewing™ Your Dreams: Inside the Mind of Alix Graham-Michel

TV Personality, Educational Consultant, Interior Decorator

*"Keep your passion and your dream.
It's okay to put it on the back burner
for a little while, but never let the fire die out."*
—Alix Graham-Michel

Thread the needle of persistence with a single thread of fascination and undying passion and you'll have what it takes to make a magic carpet that will carry you from one of the poorest nations in the world to living your dream.

Born and raised in Haiti, where her childhood passion and dream career wasn't even considered a legitimate profession, Alix Graham-Michel is a remarkable woman with an inspiring story.

From the beginning of her journey as little girl infatuated with fashion magazines to working for the United Nations in New York at the age of 25, Alix never let go of her dream. Even after becoming the proud mother of a daughter and son and enduring a bitter, devastating divorce after 25 years of marriage, she refused to give up her love affair with fashion.

Today, as an educational consultant, designer, and interior decorator she delights audiences around the world during her sewing workshops and as she regularly appears on the TV show America Sews.

THE BIRTH OF PASSION

Have you always loved sewing?

I remember sitting next to my grandmother and she used to

make so many things—all sown by hand. I was amazed at how perfect things used to turn out even though she was not using a sowing machine at that time. I was always fascinated by the fashion, the sewing—the craft.

My mother was also a seamstress so, of course she used to sew a lot. Although she had a regular job she would come home and also sew for people.

I was always there, looking. I would take some of her fabric and make clothes for my dolls. I remember when I was in school my friends would subscribe to comic books and things like that. But my subscription was to a French fashion magazine. I was fascinated by it. In fact, I made my first dress from a pattern inserted in one the magazines.

I would also go to the movie and see something I liked and sketch it. Then I would bring it to my mom and ask her to make it for me because she made my clothes. I loved to be well dressed and my mother was an excellent seamstress.

A DREAM DEFERRED

Growing up in Haiti, being a seamstress was not considered to be a profession. When we say fashion here [the U.S.] it's a big thing. But in Haiti it wasn't.

You would have to go to the university and get a degree in business, or be a doctor or an engineer. That's what they considered to be a true profession. Being a seamstress was considered to be below a profession. It's something you would do if you weren't educated. But now it's considered to be a business, a profession. It's big.

Speaking of big, you have a lot going on right now. You're a TV personality. You're an educational consultant, a designer, and an interior decorator. How did you go from working with the United Nations to doing what you do right now—A Passion for Sewing™?

When I was working at the United Nations I went to FIT [Fashion Institute of Technology in New York] because I was still fascinated by the craft. Although I was not doing it, I still wanted to explore that part of me that I loved so much. I always made my own clothes and I loved decorating.

When I was pregnant with my son, Demetri, I decided to stay home, so I never went back to FIT, but I wanted to. It was my lifelong dream. When my son was in kindergarten I saw that they were advertising for the French Fashion Academy where you could get a certificate by doing two semesters in eight months.

Were you working for the UN at that time?

No. I stopped working for the UN when my son, Demetri, was born and my daughter, Pascale, was about 4½ years old.

So, although you were a stay-at-home mom you never stopped pursuing your passion?

No, I never stopped. I made everything I wore, I decorated my home, I started designing for boutiques and I tried to get things going but, of course, my priority was my children, my family, my husband and my home. I was picky. Everything had to be nice, neat, and clean.

In order to do all of that and to do it perfectly you have to sacrifice something. What I sacrificed was a lot of the sewing and the designing.

I would talk to my husband and say "You know, I have so much in my mind that wants to come out!" It was almost painful to think that I had all of that and not be able to do something with it.

Did you ever tell yourself that you would have more time for your passion after your children were grown?

I tried to do both: take care of my family and work on my passion, but I knew that I was sacrificing my passion. I remember that my husband used to say, "You'll be able to do that when they are out of the house." But for me it was like "Oh, my God! I'm going to be so old by that time I don't think I'll be able to do it."

"I have so much in my mind that wants to come out!"

DEALING WITH THE PAIN

When you were divorced after 25 years, how did you deal with the pain?

When I got divorced I got the opportunity to work with the company I work with now [Viking Sewing Machine Group]. It was a way for me to get away from the setting, from where I used to live. So, I moved to Cleveland [Ohio] to work for the company.

I have to tell you that it was the support of my family and mainly my passion for sewing and design that got me through.

Divorced after 25 years, that's a lot of adversity to go through. That's one of the reasons that I have a tremendous amount of respect for you.

You know, I'm still hurting from it. And that's why I tell people to always keep your passion alive because I was able to channel all of my pain and frustration into my passion. It gave me a way to escape. I just dove into it.

Because of what I was going through I couldn't sleep. I would sleep for about two hours a night for the first two years after my divorce. So, I would sew for almost 24 hours a day.

I'm so passionate about what I do that when I get up in the morning the first place I go is to my [home] studio. It's my pride. The work is there, but it's easy for me. When someone calls me I say, "I'm in the dungeon."

Your dungeon, huh? That's funny.

AT LAST...A DREAM COME TRUE

So, after your divorce it the way you picked yourself up and put the pieces back together was to totally submerge yourself in the pursuit of your dream, right?

Definitely and everyday I'm amazed when I go and speak to a group. I never thought that I would be doing this. Through my passion I have touched so many people. It's unbelievable!

Also, I'm a person of great faith. I felt like God wanted show me that although you lost so much, you have another calling and through that I reach people.

One time I got this email from one of the people who were at a presentation I did in Kentucky. The email said:

"I know you won't remember me but I was sitting in front of you and the lady sitting next to me was my mother. I just want to thank you. You don't know what you did for me and for her that day. My mother used to sew a lot and she had lost her passion for it. She used to be so good at it. And as a gift for her birthday I bought her to your presentation. Since seeing you she has not stopped sewing."

When I read the email I couldn't stop crying and I felt so good. I get so much satisfaction out of things like that. I get so many emails and sometimes people drive eight hours just to come and listen to me and see all the things I'm going to show them. So, although the pain of my divorce is still there, in those moments, I leave it all behind. I forget about everything.

What do you enjoy more, sewing and designing or speaking and teaching?

All of the above.

Ha!

TURNING YOUR PASSION INTO A PROFESSION

What advice would you give someone that is interested

in turning his or her passion into a profession?

Anything that you have a passion for, you have to work hard at it. Just because it's your passion doesn't mean that you don't have to work hard.

In fact, I feel that the reason I do a good job is because I work hard at it. I renew myself all the time. I don't sit down and say okay I'll just show the same thing again this year.

These people are coming to me and I respect that. I respect them and I want them to be able to leave with a lot of information. Sometimes a person will say, "Why don't you just spend a week with me. I'm going to kidnap you!"

If I could just find somebody to pay my bills and just give me a little bit of food, I could do it for free. I don't need anything else.

Well, that's what they say about your purpose. It's something you love to do so much that you would do it for free but you do it so well that they will pay you to do it.

My thing is helping people. You have to help people because the more you help the more blessings you get.

It happens everyday for me. When I share what I know it's seems like the next day, or as I'm presenting, another idea or blessing comes to me and I say, "Oh my God. Look at that."

So, the more you share, the more you get. And you need to have good people around you that are supporting you and encouraging you. You have to stick to it and read. Get information, but make sure that what you're getting is good advice. If you have to, check with 3 or 4 different people. And lastly, don't think that you can do it all by yourself.

"The more you share, the more you get."

IN THE SPOTLIGHT

What about the TV show? How did you get your spot on America Sews?

I got that because I work with the company. They have 13 shows in a series and they have sponsors. The sponsors have the bulk of the time on the show. So, if it's a 30 minute show, they have 20 minutes, sometimes 25, and at the end of the show they have one of the educational consultants, like me, who works with the company come on to show a quick project. So, that is what I used to do.

For the past two series they have asked me to do a full show, which is great. It's not something they normally have an educator do, but people are writing in and they like what I do. So, when the host of the show called me for ideas for shows and I started giving them good ones, the lady in charge of programming suggested that I just do the whole show.

It's a privilege being asked to do a full show. It's not something they normally ask. Because they had a good response from the first show, I'm doing a second full show with them in May [2008].

OVERCOMING THE CHALLENGES

We know that dreams come with challenges. What's the most challenging thing about your career?

Hmm...for me there are challenges, but I don't consider them to be obstacles. They could have turned into obstacles, but I wouldn't let them turn into that.

When I first started I was hardly paid. It's not a highly paid craft unless you branch out into a lot of other things. I had enough money for my rent and utilities. As far as the food part goes, most of the time I was traveling so that was a [reimbursable] expense. I'm on my own right now and I can easily take care of myself. I don't have anything to throw away, but it's profitable.

And most importantly, it's what you love to do.

Yes. When I joined the company it wasn't very big. Now it is. At first I was the only black person in the whole company in a position like mine. I was traveling throughout the United States to a lot of different parts of the country. But I have to tell you that it was all positive for me because I know who I am and that's what helped me.

I had a wonderful upbringing where my parents taught me, as I taught my children, to just be yourself and do your best. So, if you know what you're talking about and you know it's the right thing then you shouldn't worry about it. There were a few people that acted negatively towards me, but I didn't let it affect me.

MANAGING REGRETS AND WEAKNESSES

If there were one thing that you could change about your life today what would it be?

I would have wanted to be a little bit younger. I would have wanted to start earlier. Maybe by now I would have had about 20 books. That's my ultimate dream—to write a book. But I am a perfectionist and I always thought that I had to do so much more.

For instance, there were a lot things that I made that I took out and showed people and they would change one little thing and the next thing you know they would have a book. If I knew then what I know now, I would be sitting on the French Riviera sipping Champagne and eating caviar!

So, in other words you don't have to wait for everything to be perfect because in doing so someone else could be capitalizing on your ideas or similar ideas.

Yes. You have to take a chance. Perfection is my weakness or flaw. Also, I don't like criticism because I know all of my flaws and I'm highly critical of myself. That keeps me behind.

I could have taken more risks. I could have said to myself, "Okay so I did it and there were like two mistakes, so what?" Instead, I will look at something over and over. Then do it again and wait. So, at times this causes me to take two steps instead of five.

At least you can acknowledge your weaknesses and flaws. Many people can't and self-awareness is important to success.

LIVING *YOUR* DREAM

Unfortunately, there are a lot of people who have dreams, talents, and abilities that they never realize. So, as we bring this to a close let's sum everything up with one final question. What does it take to live your dream?

When you have a dream you have to think about your inner self. This part of me is so real. It gives me pleasure. At times I would think I could have been so far in my quest for my passion, but I made a sacrifice for my family and for me it was worth it.

So, I know that people have responsibilities and sometimes they go into a field that does not leave them fulfilled. But you should keep your passion and your dream. It's okay to put it on the back burner for a little while, but never let the fire die out.

"You have to help people because the more you help the more blessings you get."

Chanell St. Junious, B.S., J.D.

Chanell St. Junious is an anomaly; a Visionary, whose ingredients include Attorney, Artist, and Scribe. Her history resounds much like an old blues song tinged with an unexpectedly invigorating chorus.

As a child, Chanell developed a love affair with words... spoken, written, whispered...words. She used reading as a temporary escape from poverty and uncertainty.

Upon graduating high school, Chanell joined the United States Army. After serving in Desert Storm, she left the military to pursue an undergraduate degree at Southern University in Baton Rouge, Louisiana. A four year journey took almost eight years due to her lack of dedication and focus. Before receiving her Bachelor of Science degree, she accepted a career position at the United States Post Office. Five years later, she found herself constantly battling feelings of stagnation. No matter what changed, the two constants in her life had been her love of words and heart for advocacy. As such, she applied to Southern University Law Center. Surprisingly, she was admitted. In the fall of 2002 she resigned from career position of six years to pursue her life long dream of becoming an attorney.

Now over thirty years old, the nontraditional student began the challenging three year climb. The strain of law school and the demanding transitions of life were balanced by her love of reading and skill as a writer. In 2005, Chanell graduated from the Law Center with the honor of Cum Laude, finishing in the top ten percent of her class. She relocated to Georgia and began preparation for the bar. Needing a diversion from countless pressures, Chanell began writing poetry. The "diversion" quickly became a passion.

After passing the Georgia Bar, Chanell accepted a position as an Assistant Public Defender for Newton County in Georgia, USA. She also embraced her gifting, becoming a spoken word artist, song writer, and novelist. She now operates her own law firm, **Chanell M. St. Junious, P.C.** and will be releasing her first book of poetry in the fall of 2008.

Chanell M. St. Junious, P.C.
1182 B Washington Street
Covington, Georgia 30014
Tel: 770-385-4697
www.stjuniouslaw.com

VIII.
The Case for Living Your Dreams: Inside the Mind of Chanell St. Junious, J.D.

Attorney, veteran, writer, spoken word artist

*"Marry your purpose and your vision
and then translate it into dollars."*
–Chanell St. Junious

Take a soldier, a writer, a spoken word artist, a lawyer, and a divorced, single mom; squeeze them into one mind and one body and you will have a new twist on the term Renaissance Woman. You'll have a woman with a powerful presence and a bold spirit. You will have Chanell St. Junious.

Creative and driven, Chanell has made her share of mistakes and bad choices like the rest of us. But in her words, "time isn't wasted as long as you learn the lesson. If you don't learn the lesson, you're just burning up daylight."

The eldest of three siblings from the small rural town of Lake Arthur, Louisiana, Chanell has learned many lessons in her eventful life. Although her courage and commitment have continuously been put on trial, she remains undaunted and has won the case for living her dreams.

LOVE AND SACRIFICE

After high school, you joined the army. Did you join because you wanted to or because you weren't sure about what to do?

It's funny how that transpired. I was a good student and a good athlete, but my family was poor. My parents got divorced when I was in the tenth grade so, we moved in with my grandmother. We went from being middle class to being really poor.

I didn't know about grants and since my mother was a public servant who helped everybody I didn't feel comfortable going to her and asking, "How are we going to do this?"

So, what I decided is that I was going to go into the military because I didn't want her to have to give me money and take money away from my siblings while I was in school.

So, actually, you joined the Army to sacrifice for your family.

Yes. Exactly. But I didn't tell her that until right before I got out.

What did she say when you told her?

She was moved. She cried. She was appreciative, but she was really hurt. I got some scholarships, but even on scholarship you would want to be able buy clothes and go to McDonald's. I didn't want to put that kind of pressure on her.

PLAYTIME IS OVER

In your bio you mentioned that you lacked focus and you were uncommitted. How did you come to realize that it was time to stop playing and get down to business?

I don't think there was one "ah-ha moment" for me. A lot of it was that I didn't think I could do it. And I was afraid to want it just in case I failed.

How did you get over that?

I just kept "walking" and I began to know who I was as a person. And I got married during that time. Subsequently, I was divorced, but I got married while getting my under graduate degree. And that helped me to focus as well. As I began to know myself I began to accept my capabilities—what I was really able to do versus what I thought I could.

That's important because many get confused and are frequently unable to make that distinction. People end up selling them selves short.

Exactly.

THE LITTLE ATTORNEY THAT COULD

How did you become interested in practicing law?

From the time I was a kid, if there was some type of dispute on the schoolyard. *"Such and such"* is fighting with this one or that one and I would get in the middle of it. I would always advocate for the person whom I thought was being wronged.

That never stopped. Even during my time at the Post Office— I was one of the younger people who had a career position—I was always in the middle of something, trying to fix something. Whether it was someone's marital problems or issues with management, I was always in the thick of trying to fix things. That's who I am.

You were on the schoolyard trying to break up fights. Ha! I grew up in Philly where that could be a dangerous habit.

And it was dangerous! I had a lot people who wanted to fight with me because of that. But it was what it was.

People would ask me what I wanted to be and I would say, "I want to be a lawyer." But it was something that was elusive for me. I didn't know any black attorneys and there were none in my family. I wanted to be a lawyer, but it seem like it was impossible.

So, the first thing you had to do was convince yourself that it was possible. You had to get yourself to say, "I think I can."...like *The Little Engine that Could.*

Yes. And on top of that I was thinking to myself, "It took you eight years to finish undergrad. How are you going to go to law school?" So, there were a lot mental things that I had to overcome within myself.

There wasn't a process. It was more like: "You know you have

to do better than this. You know you have to do what you're sup-
posed to be doing with your life. Just try. If they let you in, we'll
see what happens."

**"You know you have to do better than this.
You know you have to do what you're
supposed to be doing with your life."**

TRANSFORMATION AND REBIRTH

**When you finally decided to pursue your law degree, you
were in your thirties. Most people are afraid to go after
their dreams, especially at that point in their life. How did
you convince yourself to do what you love to do?**

For me, it was not an option. Everywhere I go I tend to move to
the forefront. It's not an intentional thing it's just the way that it
happens. I had been at the Post Office for seven years and I felt
like I was dying. I really did.

I had helped everybody that I could help. I was on the man-
agement track. They wanted me to do this and do that. But the
reality was, I felt like I was literally dying. Minus the conversa-
tions I had with the people at work, there was nothing challeng-
ing me in any way, shape, or form.

I was stagnant. I wasn't growing and I wasn't moving. I was in
a system that was not goal oriented. It didn't matter if I did my
job well or poorly I was going to get a raise on April 15th so, my
mind was becoming dull. I got sucked into it because they pay
well. The money was good so, I was able to attain the things I
wanted financially. But I was dying.

I don't knock the system. It provides a great living for a lot of
people. The Post Office gave people, black people especially, a
chance to go from below the poverty level to living very well. A
lot of people I knew weren't college educated, but they were able
to compete financially because of those jobs. But it wasn't for me

and I had to go.

So, for you it wasn't really about getting over your fear. It was about being totally and utterly disgusted and realizing that it was time to move on.

Yeah.

LIVING *YOUR* LIFE

What advice would give someone that wants to turn his or her passion into a profession?

The first thing I'd say is to be honest with yourself about what that passion is. A lot of times we act like something is our passion because people tell us it is. You have to make sure that you're being true to yourself. Make sure that you're not living a life just because someone you trust has told you that's what you should be doing. That's the first thing.

Let's touch on that a little. So, you're saying that a person has to make sure that someone else's dream isn't superimposed on his or her life, right?

That's exactly what I'm saying. And the other thing I would say is: marry it. Whatever that thing is, marry it. Marry your purpose and your vision and then translate it into dollars.

"A lot of times we act like something is our passion because people tell us it is... Make sure that you're not living a life just because someone you trust has told you that's what you should be doing."

THE PEACEFUL SOLDIER

What was your most challenging or memorable moment from serving in Desert Storm?

The challenge was just actually going over there. I was really young—eighteen. I'm from a small town. I didn't join the military to go to war. The entire time we were on our way there, I just kept thinking to myself, "We are not going to Iraq. We can't be going to Iraq!"

When I got off the plane and saw the desert I was like, "Oh, my God! We are actually in Iraq." It was an amazing experience. The one thing that I can say that might sound crazy is that it was the most peaceful time in my life.

What made that period of time so peaceful?

Because I had made peace with God and accepted the fact that there was a possibility I was going to die. And once I accepted that I really got to just live for the first time and to be at peace with myself and everything that was going on around me. It's funny...the things that you can see, sense, and experience once you've made peace about an issue.

Unfortunately, most people never find that kind of peace. What do think causes people to miss out on that type of peace?

I think that we don't accept things, whatever they maybe. We don't sit down and make peace with things like: I'm an attorney and I'm going to have my own firm. And so, whatever comes along with that—the challenges, the struggles, or whatever—you have to suck it up and drive on because it's what you've decided to do.

That type of peace doesn't come to me now because I'm constantly in motion, my mind is constantly going. I'm always thinking about what the next step is instead of appreciating the moment. That's why I take Fridays off. In my other jobs I couldn't do that. I was hard charging and stressed out. So, Friday is just my day to do nothing if that's what I choose.

So you have a different reason for saying "Thank God it's

Friday."

Amen. Yes indeed.

Thank God it's My Friday!

Yes! My Friday.

"It's funny...the things that you can see, sense, and experience once you've made peace about an issue."

THE LAW IS HARD ON THE SOUL

What area of law do you practice?

I specialize in criminal defense, but I also do family law which includes *guardian ad litem* work and divorces. I do juvenile matters. I don't do bankruptcy or real estate.

What's the most challenging thing about being an attorney?

The most challenging thing about being an attorney is that the work pulls at my soul. Criminal law is what broke me in. I was an Assistant Public Defender for Newton County [Georgia].

Having to be in that criminal element everyday—seeing people making poor choices everyday, and seeing what the court system does and how the jail is run—having to deal with that daily. Sometimes for eight hours per day—actually more like ten hours per day—the criminal element really wore down my soul.

I couldn't control how I dealt with that which is why I decided to have my own practice. There was more that I wanted to do and there were certain areas I didn't want to touch. I wanted to have more control over how I navigated through the legal system.

That personal element was hard for me. You're still a person that is affected by the things that you see. But you have to act like you're not affected when you are advocating on behalf of people.

THE ATTORNEYPRENEUR

Since you have your own practice there's an entrepreneurial hat that you also wear. What's the most challenging thing about having your own practice and being an entrepreneur?

I'd have to say going out and drumming up your own business. I've also been a visionary since I was kid. I was blessed. Although we're divorced now, my husband, who was a businessman, really helped me develop my business acumen. Having that inside of me and having someone around that was business oriented fed that part of me.

So, I enjoy the business. The part that's challenging is the commission. If I'm not getting enough calls or generating enough clients, I don't like that.

CLIENTS, STRESS, AND PRESSURE—OH, MY!

When you're feeling the stress and pressure of not having enough clients how do you deal with it? How do you deal with adversity?

That's a good question. How do I deal with it? I pretty much just sit down and asses what my needs are. You have to have a goal. If you're striking at the air and doing things aimlessly you are going to wear yourself out.

I may say to myself, "I need two more clients this week." So, I hit the street and start passing out business cards. I talk a lot. So, when people figure out that I'm an attorney it generally leads to them asking questions or saying that there is something that I can do for them. Whatever the case may be, it's just setting a goal and then going out there and making it happen.

When you're out attacking that goal does it alleviate some of the stress and pressure?

No, absolutely not! I still have to get a client.

So, you feel the stress and pressure and just concentrate on getting it done?

Yes. And when I need a diversion, I write. Writing is what takes away the pressure for me.

**"You have to have a goal.
If you're striking at the air and doing things
aimlessly you are going to wear yourself out."**

MS. MOM, ATTORNEY AT LAW

You're an attorney with your own practice and you're a single mom. What's the most challenging thing about being a single mom?

Being a single parent I feel a tremendous amount of pressure knowing that I'm raising two black women in the society we live in today. Also, I'm trying to have enough balance where I am. Not just being an attorney advocating for other people, but being a mom that's giving my children the best of me and not someone else the best of me.

So, when I do what I do, I try to keep that in mind. That's a tremendous amount of pressure because as a writer and an attorney you see all of the issues that are pertinent to women. You see the affects of bad parenting when these girls grow up and do all of this insane stuff.

How do your daughters feel about mommy being an attorney?

They love it. My 4-year old is enthralled with the criminal side of things. She's constantly asking about the cases and about the people. She's always asking, "Why did they do that?" It's great because I can actually have intellectual conversations with them about what I'm doing. My oldest daughter is just as proud as she could be.

FULLY REGRET FREE

It sounds as if in spite of a few errors and some challenges, you've had a good life. Is there anything thing you would change about your life right now? If so, what would it be?

I don't' think I would change anything because if I changed anything I wouldn't know as much as I know. I wouldn't be as appreciative as I am. I wouldn't be as wise as I am. Every experience was needed. Do I wish I didn't have to go through the pain I went through associated with the decisions that I made? Of course, but I wouldn't change who I am right now for anything.

So, the nugget of wisdom that comes from what you're saying is: it's okay to wish you had done better, but do not live a life full of regrets.

Yes, because the time isn't wasted as long as you learn the lesson. If you don't learn the lesson you're just burning up daylight. If you misstep so be it. But learn the lesson.

Where will Chanell St. Junious be in the next five years?

Five years from now I will likely be a judge, but not for ever. I will likely have writing as one of my primary money-making tools because writing is indeed my passion. I'm going to do film and plays and books. I'll be speaking a lot because I think I'm going to be in the political arena as well. Five years from now is going to be beautiful!

What's the most important thing to remember about living your dreams?

The thing to remember is that life is really short. It's a gift. Life is too short too waste on being miserable about a job or a relationship or anything that is not feeding you and helping you to grow. So, don't waste your time. Every minute is not going to be productive, but realize that whether you do what you're supposed to or not, the time is going to pass.

What about some spoken word? Do you have a poem about achieving your dreams or overcoming adversity that you can leave with us?

What? So, you're just going to put me on the spot like that?!

Yes!

(Turn the page to check out Chanell's poem.)

The Inevitable
by Chanell St. Junious

Whispers...
Urging me
to do "this"
Yearnings I can't
dismiss
As just some phase
Visions invading my days
Coloring me different...
The world labels me
A "Success"
While my want
leaves me distant
Powerless to
resist this... change
Too Afraid
that my life
will stay the same
So I...
accept this forced
Transition
"My" plans resounded so loudly
That I almost missed it...
Greatness refuses
to Wait any longer...
The cries of my destiny
Getting stronger...
doubt almost convinced me
that it was too late...
But Eternity whispers
"Now..."
As My fate
refuses...
to wait

Kendall Clark—Prosperity Partners, Inc.

Early in life, Kendall knew he wanted to become an entrepreneur. The opportunity presented itself in the fall of 1999 when he started a Home-Based Business and in 2003 developed Prosperity Partners, Inc.

Being an avid reader of books on leadership, networking and communication, he attributes this to the success in his own business where he has been recognized for achieving personal sales of over 1,300 and averaging 30+ sales per month. He has spoken to and inspired audiences on various topics such as Leadership, Goal Setting, Success and Motivation, Sales, Team Building, Identity Theft, and Entrepreneurship. Kendall has also built a successful networking team where he is currently leading thousands of independent business owners through the daily challenges of business ownership.

Currently, Kendall is very involved in other speaking and networking groups such as Toastmasters International and BNI (Business Network International) where he recently served as President. He also enjoys traveling the country speaking to over 100,000 high school students on the importance of maintaining good grades in preparation for college and to the parents on the different funding strategies for college. Some of his clients have included: Bowie State University, City of Norfolk, William and Mary, Towson University, Penn State University, Pomona College, Norfolk State University, Hampton University, St. Paul College, William E. Woods, Hampton Roads Leadership Conference, National Association Of Student Councils, Granby High, Bethel High, Woodbridge High, and Yorktown High just to name a few.

Kendall is also the host of The H.A.P.S. Radio Show in which he interviewed some of the top unsigned artist in the industry. Kendall has also coauthored his first book *Unleash the Greatness Within You.*

To have Kendall speak at your next event contact him through:
Email: theprosperitypartners@yahoo.com or
Directly: (757) 515-2220

IX.
Don't Wake Me.
I Haven't Finished Dreaming.

By Kendall Clark

How happy would you be if you were actually living your dreams—knowing that you were doing what God called you to do?

How about relentlessly following your passions and living your purpose?

Waking up everyday excited about beginning a new day and expecting new opportunities?

Do you long for this type of satisfaction?

Is it really possible to live a life of purpose and passion? To have a career you love, instead of a job you hate?

Are you relegated to live a life long nightmare or is it really possible to live your dreams?

I believe you can find your true passion and purpose, which will put you in line to live your dreams. It has been a journey to get to this point in my life. I have made mistakes and bad choices, but with each mistake I have learned and grown as a person. During this journey of positioning myself to live my dreams, I have gone through nearly losing my house, having a car repossessed, seeing my six figure income cease, and enduring arguments and strife with my spouse and immediate family members.

As I went through each experience, I was constantly bombarded by thoughts of failure, wondering whether I was really living my dreams or more of a nightmare. I constantly asked myself: "Is living my dream this hard?" "Is following my purpose this difficult?" "Why can't anyone see what I am trying to do?"

I shed many tears asking God, "Why me?" Eventually, I recognized that no one promised that living my dreams would be easy.

If it were easy, more people would be deriving joy from their lives and careers, instead of being discontent—living for Fridays and hating Mondays, counting the days until the next the holiday when they would be off, only to spend that day dreading having to go to work the next day to a job they utterly despised.

No one promised that living my dreams would be easy.

DESPERATE TIMES

Nine years ago, when I began the path to living my dreams, I was at a job that I hated. I was under enormous pressure. I had just taken over as point person for a unit that was severely backlogged. That was problematic as any delay would cost the government millions of dollars.

I was so overstressed and near the brink of despair that I elected to have surgery that I had put off for years, just so I wouldn't have to go to work. I know it sounds far fetched, but desperate times called for desperate measures. I was out on sick leave for three months. During that time, I asked myself an earnest question—do I want to continue living this nightmare for thirty more years or do I want to follow my dreams? I chose the latter.

FROM BIG MONEY TO BIG PROBLEMS

My wife and I started a business in the field of network marketing. We did quite well and quickly worked our way to the top tier of the company. We were recognized for being in the top three percent of income earners and among their top producers/recruiters. At one point, we had over 1,300 personal customers. We went from earning just over $2,000.00 a month to over

$14,000.00 a month.

After five years of building the business, the unexpected happened—one of our largest group accounts laid off four hundred people, which resulted in a substantial reduction of our income. I was near the point of going back to a more common routine of employment; however, I was still searching for something to develop my talents.

While we had our network marketing business, I often had to travel and train associates. I remember one training in particular where I was talking to about 200 representatives in Detroit. That's were I discovered my passion for speaking. At that point, I set another goal and looked for opportunities to pursue my dream of entrepreneurship as a motivational speaker.

I researched online and found a plethora of information on the field. One day, my wife came across a job posting looking for motivational speakers. It was ideal; however, **it was less than two hours before the deadline** and I had to create a DVD, develop a resume, and complete the application. I applied and was chosen to attend training in Cincinnati, Ohio in July. The only problem was that I needed money "NOW" to take care of my family. Our former six-figure income producing business was now hemorrhaging profits and our savings was quickly dwindling.

THE ACCIDENTAL GENERAL MANAGER

One day to help keep me focused on my dream, I went into a local Hummer dealership to look at the model H2, which at the time was one of my dream cars. After a casual conversation, the General Manager asked if I had ever sold cars before. I hadn't nor had the thought ever crossed my mind. Curious as to how I would score, the GM asked if I would be willing to take a personality test. I humored him, took the test, and went home.

The GM called me later that day to share that I scored higher than any of his current sales people and wanted to offer me a position. I politely informed him that car sales wasn't for me. He responded by telling me that he wanted to train me to be a General Manager. Of course, I would have to start as a salesman, but in a month I would be a used car dealership manager.

I still insisted on declining the generous offer.

A few weeks went by, and after much thinking and praying, I decided to give him a call back. He told me I could start the next day. My first day there, in lieu of my training, I was immediately put on the sales floor. I had never sold cars before, but sold an H3 Hummer to my first customer. My tenacious sales attitude left an impression among the veteran sales staff.

STAYING FAITHFUL TO TRUE LOVE

After nearly two weeks, the twelve hour work days—in June nonetheless—were becoming unbearable. I was getting home exhausted and only seeing my children after they had gone to bed.

The speakers' training in Cincinnati was quickly approaching; however, with my new schedule, I would not be able to attend without the risk of losing my job. Once again, I had to make a decision. The closer the training got, the more I wanted to attend. Ultimately, I decided to leave the dealership. I was fueled by thoughts of missed time with my family and the various engagements I wanted to attend, but couldn't because I had to work.

The next day, I informed my mentor at the dealership, of my plans to resign. He tried to persuade me to stay by enticing me to think of my potential income. He was missing the entire point of my resignation.

It was not merely about the money; it was about being happy and living my dreams.

My mentor was the top sales person at the dealership and was on pace to earn about $25,000 for the month of June, which did not include bonuses. My mentor and the GM often commented that I was a better salesman than he was and that I could easily exceed what he was projected to earn. This was a very tempting proposition, but joy and ease of mind were not for sale.

I resigned that day and never looked back.

As a result of that decision, I went to Cincinnati for the speakers' training, and now travel the country, pursuing my purpose and living my dreams, as a motivational speaker. In three years, I have traveled to 25 states and spoken to over 100,000 high school and college students. Not to mention the various keynote addresses, conferences, radio shows, and other trainings I conduct annually. I coauthored my first book *Unleash the Greatness Within You* and am now writing in this book, *Get ALL Fired Up! About Living Your Dreams*.

Joy and ease of mind were not for sale.

IT'S NOT EASY, BUT IT'S YOUR TURN

I am a testament that following your dreams is never easy, that you will have distractions along the way, and that you will definitely have to persist in spite of those around you who question your sanity as you step out on faith to live your dreams.

Always be mindful that when people tell you that you can't do something, it is often because they cannot see themselves doing it.

To help you live your dreams, it is important for you to "write your vision" (Habakkuk 2:2). Write out the Top 50 goals that you want to achieve over a lifetime. Then, extract and concentrate on your Top 5 one-year goals. Write a paragraph for your Top 5 goals, detailing what it will mean to you to reach them. To reach your dreams, you may have to shed tears and endure seasons that seem nightmarish. During those times, keep in the forefront of your mind that it may take some work to live your dreams and remember:

The only time success comes before work is in the dictionary.

Stay persistent in your hope. Don't you dare wake up to someone else's reality until you have finished dreaming the sweet dreams that give you life. And once last thing...

Don't wake me because I haven't finished dreaming.

NEVER STOP DREAMING

Michelle Matteson—"The Maven of Mind Marketing"

 After building and selling two successful businesses experiencing explosive growth, Michelle Drum Matteson is well acquainted with the stress, pressure, and challenges entrepreneurs face in creating their dreams. Her interest and expertise in business development began 20 years ago as a subcontractor in the industrial manufacturing field. She owned a plant operated by twenty employees. During that same time period Michelle opened a popular salon and spa called The Razor's Edge.

From the experiences gained as a business woman in a primarily male dominated industry, Michelle has developed a nation wide following for her popular workshops and seminars designed for women in the fields of business development, sales and marketing, social networking, and the art of Corporate Persuasion.

A licensed trainer for The Psychology of Persuasion and a Master Neuro-linguistic Programming Practitioner, Michelle is also the Director of Business Development for a multi-state On-Site Industrial Workforce Management and Professional Recruitment Corporation.

Michelle may be contacted at www.staffsolutions.biz or www.michellematteson.com

X

Listen to the Voice of Your Dreams
Inside the Mind of Michelle Matteson
Entrepreneur, Neuro-linguist, Professional Speaker

*"We have to calm that critical inner voice
that we use to put ourselves down..."*
—Michelle Matteson

For most people owning one successful business would be a dream come true. But what if you owned two thriving businesses and at the height of it all you sold both of them and retired early—very early?

If you can picture that then you have an idea of what it's like to be Michelle Matteson. Enterprising, tenacious, and vibrant, once Michelle decides she's going to do something she won't let anything stand in her way. Although she excels in the often cutthroat world of business, she is kind-hearted and loves helping people. That's a rare combination.

Michelle has accomplished more in one lifetime than most people could accomplish in two and she still isn't done! Looking at her life brings a question to mind:

Who ever said that you could only live one dream?

THE HAND OF OPPORTUNITY

Tell me a little bit about your life right before you became a business owner and your transition into becoming an entrepreneur.

That's been over 20 years ago! You're stretching my memory, Al. I was working as a nurse, actually. I was working as a nurse up until the late '80's or early '90's. How I happened into business is a lesson for anybody. The opportunity presented itself and it was kind of scary for me because I had never done anything like that. When opportunity puts its hand out you can either, take the hand and go with it or pass it up.

YOU NEVER KNOW...GIVE IT A TRY

I owned some land and a company that was coming in from the east was looking for some land to put a small manufacturing plant on. They had to access some of my land, so I gave them easement to get to the land that they had bought. We got acquainted that way and during the process they came to me and said, "We are a brand new company. We have this project that we can't do in our own plant now. It's just simple assembly work. Do you think you'd like to do this on the side?"

I said, "Okay. Tell me what to do."

They handed me some plans and said, "This is what we need. Can you figure it out?"

The temptation was to respond, "No, I'm too busy." But something inside of me was intrigued and I thought, "Why not?" So, I guess the message I hope to get across is: don't ignore those little ticks that say, "You know, this could be interesting." Even if you don't know, give it a try. You never know how that's going to develop.

TENACITY, COURAGE, AND A LITTLE VOICE

I remember this part well. I had this big machine shed because we farmed at the time—this was with my former husband. I remember spreading these diagrams out on the floor, trying to figure out how to put all of this together. My husband was very busy with farming so, he didn't want anything to do with it. He said, "If you want to do it, you figure it out." So, I was tenacious in trying to figure out how to put all of these small parts together and trying to assemble this and that.

Well to make a very, very long story short—I figured out how to do it and it grew into a small, but very profitable business with twenty employees. Throughout that process I learned that I really did have a good bent for business. So, the lesson is: develop the tenacity and the courage to listen to that little voice inside of you that says, "You know, this might be something."

As my business grew I decided—just of the fun of it—to see if I could open a business that I knew nothing about, like I did the first time. Only this time, I really did know what I was doing...or I hoped I did! So, I opened a salon and spa [The Razor's Edge] from scratch. I didn't know anything about it. I certainly don't do hair and I'm not a cosmetologist or anything like that. I opened it with the intent to sell it within 5-7 years if I made it profitable and I did. So, that's a short synopsis of the past twenty years of my life.

"Develop the tenacity and the courage to listen to that little voice inside of you."

LISTEN TO YOUR INNER SELF

So, life was great. You had two profitable businesses and then you decided to sell them. How did you come to realize that it was time to sell your businesses?

I knew about two years ahead of time that I was going to sell. As any entrepreneur will tell you—and you know this yourself, Al—when you work for yourself you are harder on yourself than anybody could ever be. I was working long, long hours keeping both businesses going. I didn't have a clue that the spa and salon would grow as quickly as it did. It became another full time job. So, I was running two very fast paced businesses by myself and I knew that I was reaching a burnout point, but I didn't want to burnout. I could feel that saturation point coming.

It was the constant pressure of running two businesses that had grown to a point where I needed to either let go of the reigns and let them grow bigger or sell them. That's a hard decision and I don't know if you'll ever know if you've made the right one. But

I do know that I listened to that little voice inside that said, "You're getting very close to burnout and it's time to step back." So, that is what prompted that decision. I think it was a good one.

During the two years after I sold the businesses I came to another epiphany and listened to another small voice. So, I guess my theme here is: listen to your intuition.

CALMING YOUR INNER CRITIC

You have a whole lot of voices running around in your head!

Yeah, I know! The self-talk that we give ourselves isn't always the best because we are harder on ourselves than other people are. So, sometimes those voices are saying, "You can't do this." But you have to train yourself to step back and look at yourself from the inside. Understand your strengths and your weaknesses.

We have to calm that critical inner voice that we use to put ourselves down or to justify not trying something new or to keep ourselves from facing tough decisions. Although I made it into a two year process to make sure that everything went well, selling both of the businesses was a very scary step for me because I didn't know what was going to be on the other side. I had to look at myself from the inside with as much goodness as possible.

DEFINE YOUR DREAM AND AVOID SELF-SABOTAGE

How did you convince yourself to do what you love to do and to go after your dreams?

First, you have to clearly define what your dream is. People will come up to me and say, "I want to do what you did." And in turn I'll ask, "What exactly do you want to do?" And they give me some kind of vague concept. It's okay to have a vague concept, but you have to go after that vagueness and start chunking it down. Try new things and be realistic about the time involved.

Be goal-oriented and practice in little bits how to avoid self-sabotage when it comes to time management and unrealistic dreams. Take a step back and really look at your dream and ask, "Is this something that just makes me feel better when I think about it for awhile or do I have this driving urge inside of me?" There's a big difference there. It really does take drive and it really does take time management and focus.

And you're going to have to sacrifice something somewhere to achieve your dream. Where people get discouraged or where they don't want to take that extra leap is when their life is so full already that they wonder what areas of their life are they going to have to give up? That's a decision that people have to make, but I think that self-sabotage is probably the biggest thing to conquer.

"You're going to have to sacrifice something somewhere to achieve your dream."

EXPLORE WITH COURAGE AND PURPOSE

What should a person do first?

I think the first thing is trying many different avenues to find out what your dream consists of. A lot if times people say they want to do something, but they don't know what it takes to do it. So, taking a class, reading books, going to seminars, talking to people like you [Al Duncan], and really taking some steps towards figuring out what they really want to do about that dream. All of these things that I'm saying, I've done in some form.

Chasing after your dream without putting a lot of thought into it isn't good, but on the flip side of that, people can self-sabotage themselves by wanting to have all of their ducks in a row before they start going after their dreams. You have to have the courage to strike out, but you also have to strike out with purpose.

You may go after one avenue and realize that's not the way, so you try something else. Continuously have that focus toward your dream and don't be afraid to try things and don't be afraid to fail. I've failed at many things, but each failure helped me to learn. And I took it in context and said, "You know what? This didn't work out this time, so I'll try a different avenue or a different way." Having the courage to do that is a big step.

AN EXAMPLE OF NOT BEING AFRAID TO FAIL

Give me an example of not being afraid to fail.

When I had the salon and spa because we were a holistic spa we more like an alternative spa. We offered different types of holistic therapy. One of my friends was involved in hypnosis. I thought, "That's not being done in my area." And it interested me.

So, again, back to what I told you earlier, it sparked my interest, so I started learning all that I could about it. I read books, went to seminars, and finally decided to take some hypnosis training for myself. I became a Certified Hypnotist and incorporated that practice into my spa. From there I started developing my niche, which is a form of hypnosis that I call Waking Hypnosis. It works extremely well for helping people to stop smoking.

When I was a brand new hypnotist I was very enthusiastic and I thought I could cure anything. One of my first clients wanted to stop smoking. I was very eager and I had just learned a new technique called the Direct Dry technique.

At first, I was using whatever room was empty for my clients. And the room that was empty was right next to where my three massage therapists were. So, I had a client in the room. She was a woman with a big, husky, deep voice like a long-time smoker sometimes gets.

Part of this technique required the client to repeat what you said fifteen times silently inside of their head. So, I was all into it and I forgot to mention the critical word—silently. So, she started to bellow at the top of her lungs, "I am now and forever a non-smoker!!!" She was yelling and I was yelling it back at her. We were both yelling at the top of our lungs. I realized what was going on in the middle of it, but I thought to myself, "I am not going to stop because she's really into this. " I was having visions of my massage therapists in the other going, "Oh, my God!"

I was trying to get out of the way before the massage therapists came out, but we all came out at the same time. One of my massage therapists was glaring at me, but her client came out and said, "You know I'm a smoker and I don't even feel like smoking now!"

HA!

So, it's okay to make mistakes.

THERE'S THAT LITTLE VOICE AGAIN

Did hypnosis lead to you being a speaker and trainer? What made you realize that speaking and training were your new passions?

It did because of the organization through which I became trained as a hypnotist—The National Guild of Hypnotists. Every year they have a national conference with well over 2000 people in attendance from all over the world. People can apply to speak and give classes.

The first couple of conventions that I went to I said to myself, "I would love to be able to do that. I want to talk to a room full of people." But when I thought about it, my stomach instantly clenched and I was thinking that there was no way I could do that. The little voice inside of me asked, "Well...why not? But what would I speak about and even if I did who would listen to me?"

Finally, I just decided to do it. So, I wrote a proposal and sent it in. Never in my wildest dreams did I think that out of the hundreds of applications I would be one of the people chosen, but I was. After they chose my proposal I was like "Oh my God! Now what am I going to do?"

SCARED? DO IT ANY WAY

Now you would actually have to do it, huh?

I can't even tell you how many times I thought about calling them and saying, "I can't do this. I don't know what I'm doing." I was so nervous that I threw up in the hotel room about an hour before I was supposed to speak, but I did it. And although I had no idea how to do one, I did a PowerPoint that day. I was scarred to death, but forcing yourself to do something that absolutely terrifies you and facing your fears is probably the best thing that you could do for yourself in the long run because once you do something that seems so terrifying, nothing else is quite as bad.

I survived and even got really good reviews. So, ten years ago that's what sparked my interest in speaking and it grew from there. And I didn't have a specific message at first. I spoke about how to incorporate hypnosis in to a spa. From that came more presentations on business development, sales, and marketing and that's what I speak on now with an emphasis on subconscious communication and marketing.

It all began with a very diffuse and scary dream, but I did it. I just did it. So, I don't care how scary it is to you, just do it. Try a part of it and it's okay if you throw up.

Actually, if you throw up you happen to be in great company because Winston Churchill and many other great orators also threw up before their speeches...Steven Spielberg throws up whenever he starts shooting a new movie.

Well, I don't do that any more! It was a one time thing and I don't even remember the first 10-15 minutes of that first presentation. Nothing comes easily to me.

People might pretend that things come easily or it might look like things come easily, but I don't think so. I don't believe that. And if that's the case then I think an over used platitude is apropos: "Easy come, easy go."

That's right.

> **"Facing your fears is one of the best
> things you can do for yourself
> in the long run."**

FROM DREAM BUSINESS TO DREAM JOB

So, you've got your new passion, speaking and training, but on top of that you've got a new position with a great company. You are the Business Development Manager for Innovative Staff Solutions which you say is a dream job for you. How did that come about?

I'm probably one of the few people in the world who has actually gone from owning her own businesses and working for herself to working for somebody else because I wanted to. I've laughed about that conundrum for awhile because I've had people literally say to me, "Are you nuts?!" Most people are dying to get out of their jobs and would love to own their own businesses. And I did too in the beginning.

I think things come full circle. When I took the two years off after selling my businesses, I missed the hustle and bustle. I've trained myself to be very busy and I missed the daily interaction with people so, it was a personal decision not a financial one. I also had the luxury to take the time to look for a company that would be the best fit for me.

I began an 18 month search for just the right company—a company that could utilize and appreciate my skills and that I could work with and still do my speaking and my training. I finally found the right one. The company and I "fell in love at first sight", but we did negotiate for about a month. I respected them greatly and they respected me. They gave me a deal that I would've been stupid to turn down. I do marketing and business development training for them. I love it. I get up everyday and I'm excited. Sometimes I go in an hour early and stay an hour later. People there think I'm nuts!

THE BEAUTY OF IT ALL IS HAVING A CHOICE

I can understand how that can puzzle people. You go out and get your dream and then you want to do something else? I think the beauty of it all is when the choice is yours. That's the difference. A lot of times people will shake their head because they feel like they don't have a choice, but everybody has a choice. I've certainly put in long hours and all the things that business owners do, so I've paid my dues. Now going to work is like a vacation for me. It's fun.

You just touched on a key word—choice. When you feel like you have a choice that increases your sense of autonomy and that's a powerful way to increase your spiritual, emotional, and mental well-being.

The lesson there is even if you think you don't have a choice, take a step back and look around. Talk to people, like Al Duncan and Michelle Matteson, who can let you know that you do have a choice. There are going to be some sacrifices and some hard things to deal with, but you do have a choice.

NOT WORKING IS BORING

What was the hardest thing about going back to work?

Actually, I was bored out of my gourd [mind]. I was ready to go back.

So, was it harder not to work?

Yes. I was ready. I even started working on my degree again because I had been off and on for so many years. In fact, I remember thinking to myself, "Now that I'm back in school I'll probably find that dream position." And I did. So, all of a sudden I went from being bored to rarely having a spare minute. It's exciting.

FRIENDS, RESILIENCE, AND DARK MOMENTS

How do you deal with adversity?

I think that having people in your life who you can reach out to is important. I have two women that have been my best friends for close to thirty years. You must have those types of people in your life who can help you at your darkest moments to see the points of light. Because we all—especially entrepreneurs and people going after their dreams—have some very dark moments when you are ready to give up.

The important thing for me was that I shared my dreams and passion with my two best friends, my mother, sisters, and my aunt. So, in my dark moments when everybody else is saying, "You had better just cash in your chips, sweetie." They were the ones who came to me and said, "Don't you dare give up. Find a way."

People look at my life now and say, "Wow! How lucky you are." But to get to this point I've gone through some very dark moments. And you just think back to the times when you did do something scary or impossible and you made it. And if it you didn't that time, then you can do it this time.

There's always a solution. A person can never realize her biggest dreams without the awareness that there are going to be some pretty dark moments to go with it. You have to say to yourself, "I don't know how I'm going to get there, but I'm going to keep my eye on my dreams and get there some way." You have to have inner resilience.

REGRETS? MAYBE, MAYBE NOT

Speaking of dark moments, do you have any regrets?

Of course! But overall, no because my life is what has made me who I am now. I don't know a person alive who doesn't look back on life and think, "If I knew then what I know now, I would've done things differently." But then, who knows if you would've been who you are now? I've made mistakes and done some pretty dumb things at times, so I may have regrets for certain instances. But overall, I am who I am now and I like that.

Where will Michelle Matteson be five years from now?

You come see me in five years and then you'll know!

Ha!

Well, I'll tell you where I'm going to be. My two good friends—Donald McNaughton and Ken Owens—and I have talked often about starting seminars and workshops together. Also, one of my mentors, Will Horton, has talked about all of us doing something together. So, I can feel another venture starting!

...to be continued in a future chapter of The Maven of Mind Marketing.

**"I don't know how I'm going to get there,
but I'm going to keep my eye on
my dreams and get there
some way."**

DREAM LIFE

Kenneth Cole—Next Level Marketing

Kenneth Cole founded and launched Next Level Marketing January 1, 2005, in the South East Marketplace with a mission to build a positive image for clients that reflects confidence and success. Providing Personal and Corporate Branding Services for well over 1000 clients, 10 Corporations, and 5 Small Businesses in three years since its inception, Next Level Marketing is the fastest growing client based personal branding resource vehicle in the southeast market.

Our approach

We always endeavor to build a clear picture of NLM clients' and their business that establishes trust and acceptance, while championing each and every promotional design, so it will serve a multitude of marketing and networking functions. Next Level's Style definition (Establishing Your Brand Formula) is one of our key ingredients when developing custom designs and unique marketing materials, tailor-made to fit the client, giving both personal and business identity. This distinguishes and sets apart the business professional in order to effectively market their services.

Next Level Marketing is a one-stop-suite of services that is relationship driven and allows entrepreneurs and business professionals to have more control during their development and branding process.

Our deliverables

✓ Cutting-edge marketing solutions for business and corporate professionals

Our services include:

✓ Professional photography that captures the "true client's" personality.
✓ Custom design, development, and branding (Marketing the Sizzle) that drives NLM clients' success forward, with Determination, Poise and Professionalism
✓ Quality printing for Optimal Image Resolutions of marketing materials, as well as, drop shipment (delivery) of marketing materials

The rapid growth of the company has opened the doors for Kenneth Cole who recently founded, "BiZ Card Designers", now a sister company of Next Level Marketing.

XI

Taking Your Dreams to the Next Level: Inside the Mind of Kenneth Cole

Entrepreneur, Image Branding Expert, Photo designer

*"We can get so caught up in the destination that
we lose sight of the love of what it takes
to get there and the appreciation of
how we evolve and develop
along the way."*
—Kenneth Cole

It's been said time and time again that a picture is worth a thousand words. But if Kenneth Cole is taking the shot then it's worth a million bucks. Kenneth specializes in making people look good and he's making himself and his company, Next Level Marketing, look good in the process.

After eighteen months as an under-study with top photo designer, Michael Maragia, Kenneth decided it was time to branch out on his own. Fueled by his audacious and innovative approach to photo design and image branding, his company's growth has been explosive. But through it all, Kenneth maintains that "it's not the money, it's the love of the business" that has helped him take his dreams to the Next Level.

LOVE AND REVELATION

How did you come to realize that photo designing and image branding were your passion and that you could start a business and live your dreams through them?

While working with Mr. Maragia I developed a real love for the business. He saw the aggressive marketing techniques in me and he asked me if I would like to become a business associate and market his business and what he does. From there things grew and evolved and I was in love with the business.

How did you know when it was time to break off and start Next Level Marketing?

When I saw how quickly I was able to bring all those contacts and clientele into his business. I was able to easily show them how the services being provided would benefit them and that happened very quickly. I grew a big market for him. I remember saying to myself, "Wow! I could do this for myself."

DIVERSITY IS THE NAME OF THE GAME

He had a good business and a good business model. The only downside was that he targeted a specific market—realtors. That was 95%-98% of his market.

My market is diverse. I offer similar products and services, but to a more diverse market. Whether you are a professional speaker, a trainer, a business or image consultant, a realtor, a musician, or whatever type of business, we take care of your needs in terms of image branding. We want to give people and businesses that distinctive look of value that's different from whatever and whoever is in the marketplace.

I felt that I would reach not only a broader section of the market, but I would cross the barriers into more cultures and ethnicities. Michael's business clientele was predominantly white. When you reach a diverse market and provide a wide array of services and different products, that's your opportunity to expand.

I saw the business from a different perspective and I wanted to put a different twist on things. I wanted to go after it a lot more aggressively. He used to wonder why he was limited as far as growth was concerned. That's because of being too market specific and putting all of your eggs in one basket.

"Wow! I could do this for myself."

THE ENTREPRENEUR WITHIN

How did you convince yourself to do what you love to do? Most people are afraid.

I knew I would find my niche, eventually. Then everything would be okay. I had a desire. I believe that being an entrepreneur is innate. It's something you're born with. So, I already had that capability. It was just waiting to surface. I just had to find something that had value to me, something that I would truly bond with.

ASTOUNDINGLY IMAGINATIVE

Quite often, people limit themselves in terms of their goals and aspirations. Do you see that and if so what advice would you give someone about getting past those limits so that he or she can turn his or her passion into a profession?

You have to have an open mind because when you are one dimensional it's going to be hard. You have to transcend the market and grow your services. You have to evolve. You have to be innovative and constantly thinking in a new direction. What is your market demanding? Many people are stuck in "business as usual" mode.

I knew that if I took hold of this business that it would grow and I would do something different with it. The market pretty much dictates what you need to do and which way you need to flow with your products and services.

For example, when CD's came out we had to toss the tapes. CD's were a better a product that gave you better quality. And it's what the market demanded—easier, faster, better quality. So, one product had to become obsolete.

Another thing is that you have got to stay ahead of the competition. Be creative with your products and services. If you're going to do the same old thing how are you going to take it the next level? You have to be what I call astoundingly imaginative.

**"You have to evolve.
You have to be innovative
and constantly thinking in a new direction."**

FOR THE LOVE OF THE BUSINESS

When it comes to actually achieving your dreams let's say that someone wanted start a business similar to yours or any type of business for that matter, what is the most important thing to remember?

That it's not about the destination, it's about the journey. We can get so caught up in the destination that we lose sight of the love of what it takes to get there and the appreciation how we evolve and develop along the way.

Also, you've got to clearly know your reasoning for coming into a business. Is it for the money or is it for the love of the business? We do it for the love of the business and our main priority and goal is to make clients successful. When they win, we win. So, if you go into a business primarily looking for the money as opposed to the love of the business then you're going at it wrong. Ultimately, what you do will be more rewarding if you do it for the love of the business first.

If you look at most entrepreneurs that are successful today they were not only in it for the money, they were in for the love of what they do and what they had to offer. In fact, nine times out of ten the money wasn't the issue. It was about how the services or products would benefit people and the money came later. So, go into it for the love of what you can offer, not the dollars.

**"Go into it for the love of what you can offer,
not the dollars."**

THE THRESHOLD OF SUCCESS

A lot of times people look from the outside in and all they see is the end result. They see you have a great business, that is thriving, and growing very rapidly. What they don't see are the hurdles you had to overcome to get where you are. What's the most challenging thing that you've experienced in terms of being an entrepreneur?

Staying focused. Staying focused on the vision and being determined to do what I want to do. That is not easy. The key to success lies in anyone's hand. The fact that one individual knows more than another individual has little to do with success. Success comes down to who's more determined at all costs to pursue the vision and not give up, not give in, or throw in the towel. Those individuals that are more determined are the ones that will ultimately be successful. Most people who throw in the towel were probably right at the threshold of success.

THE REAL POWER

Speaking of staying focused and making sure that you stay determined—adversity is going to come your way. So, how do you deal with it?

I take it as a grain of salt. It's an experience. It's life and it's part of business. The real power doesn't lie in the money or being wealthy. It lies the ability to be strong in the face of adversity. If you are innovative and you have that kind of strength you will surmount the wall of negativity and continue to thrive.

PATIENCE IS A VIRTUE

If there were one thing in your life that you could change, what would it be?

That's very interesting. I don't really know that there is anything I would change. Are you talking about the business or life in general?

Either one, your business is part of your life.

I can't say that I wish I would've started earlier because it wasn't time; when you find your niche, that's the time regardless of whether you're young or old. But if there was one thing that I could potentially change it would be this. Although I was open-minded, I would have thought things through a little bit slower. I would've been a little bit more patient. Having everything in front of me caused me to be so excited about the business that a few times I put the cart in front of the horse.

Where will Kenneth Cole and Next Level Marketing be in five years?

Our goal is to become more broad-based and not just dominate the southeast market but to reach markets across the country and the world. In other words, we'll be taking it to the Next Level!

"The real power doesn't lie in the money or being wealthy. It lies in the ability to be strong in the face of adversity."

DREAM BIG

Dr. Joe Teal—International Seminar Leader

Success is a science, and Dr. Joe Teal teaches the science of success. He operated his own private business in an Atlanta suburb for 14 years, and successfully retired at the young age of 45. Authors of the book The Obvious Expert, list him as one of the "top minds in consulting", and an "obvious expert advisor".

Dr. Teal has over 20 years of experience helping men and women of all ages from around the world learn how to feel better, make more money, and achieve a much happier life.

An International Seminar Leader, he has presented programs on business and personal success in Asia, the British Virgin Islands, South America (in Spanish), and all across the United States for corporations, government agencies, medical facilities, military bases, and municipalities.

Dr. Teal has been affiliated with over a dozen institutions of higher learning including being Assistant Faculty Advisor to the Dean of Behavioral Sciences at South Florida Bible College, Curriculum Advisor for International Sports at Kennesaw State University (in Atlanta), and U.S. Development Coordinator for the Philosophy Department at Central University of Ecuador.

He has served as a faculty member for other prestigious institutions such as the American Academy of Pain Management, Connecticut School of Broadcasting (Atlanta campus) and International Association of Counselors & Therapists. And he has served as a consultant for the Center For Traumatic Stress and Law Enforcement Personnel Services, Inc.

Dr. Teal maintains his international headquarters in Dallas, GEORGIA, with branch offices in Haleyville, Alabama, and Quito, Ecuador.

XII.
Get What You Want: How To Set Powerful Goals And Accomplish Seemingly Impossible Ones

By Dr. Joe Teal

"Most of us have a pretty clear understanding of the world we want. What we lack, is an understanding of how to go about getting it."
—Hugh Gibson

PREDICTING THE FUTURE

Do you know how to predict the future?

Sure you do—you've already done it many times during your lifetime. We predict the future by simply setting a goal. And we create the future, by accomplishing that goal. Haven't you ever said to yourself or others that you were going to accomplish something specific, and then you ended up doing it? First you set a goal, and then you accomplished it. You predicted and created your own future!

GOALS

Before we can adequately discuss setting and accomplishing goals, we must first define exactly what a goal is:

A Goal = A Wish + A Deadline

If you are not setting a deadline for your goals, you are only wishing.

Wishes rarely come true; goals can be accomplished.

"It takes a little courage and a lot of self-control
and some determination, if you want to reach a goal.

It takes a great deal of striving, a firm and stern-set chin;
no matter what the battle, if you're really out to win.

There's a rule of life to guide you, as you seek prosperity:
never put your wishbone, where you backbone ought to be."

—Florence Koba

WHERE ARE YOU GOING IN LIFE?

In order to effectively control the direction you are going in life, there are three important questions that must first be asked and answered in writing:

1. What Do You Really Want?

This question provides you with a sense of direction in your life. Ask yourself exactly what it is that you wish for, dream about having, or want with all your heart (regardless of what other people might think). And be specific. Exactly what would it take to make you happy? If you don't know exactly what it is that you want, or exactly what it would take to make you happy, how will you ever know when you get it? You may already have what it takes to be happy, but you just don't realize it!

2. Why Is The Goal Important To You?

If you can think of and write down enough reasons, or one big enough reason why it is important to you to accomplish your goal, it will provide you with a constant source of motivation to

succeed. If you can't think of any good reasons why it is impor-
tant to you that the goal be accomplished, then you probably
should forget about that particular goal and move on to another.
Because if you have no reason to accomplish a specific goal, you
will have no motivation to accomplish it and you will be very un-
likely to succeed.

3. When Do You Plan To Accomplish It?

We have already established that a goal is a wish + a dead-
line, and that if you are not setting a deadline for your goals you
are only wishing. Have you ever noticed how you tend to put
off work assignments that have later due dates, and take more
seriously those that are due right away? The reason is that
whenever you set a deadline for accomplishing your goal, you
create a sense of urgency, establish a priority, and put an end to
procrastination. To eliminate procrastination, set a deadline for
your goal. Then, simply honor the commitment that you made
to yourself. That's all there is to it.

Once you have determined exactly what it is that you want to
accomplish, exactly why it is important to you that it be accom-
plished, and exactly when you plan to accomplish it, the *"how"*
will automatically come to you. You will begin to literally think,
talk, eat, sleep and breathe your desire to succeed. You will be-
come more tuned-in to all the wonderful ideas and opportunities
that already exist around you.

**"The greatest thing in this world is not so much
where you stand, as in what direction
we are moving."**

—Oliver Wendall Holmes

VISUALIZE YOUR GOALS

A Treasure Map, also known as a Life Success Plan, is probably
one of the most simple and effective methods for accomplishing

goals that I have ever seen. But because it is so simple, it is very difficult to get most people to design one.

A Treasure Map is nothing more than a clean, white piece of poster paper, on which you have glued magazine pictures, photographs, or drawings that best illustrate the specific things you wish to accomplish, acquire, or become during your lifetime.

In Japan it was found that when executives planned 3-year goals in this way, they were able to accomplish those goals in only 18 months; and when they planned 5-year goals, they were able to accomplish them in only 2½ years. That's half the time it would ordinarily take! But because it was so difficult to get anyone to plan for 5 years, they only insisted that their executives plan for 3 years at the time.

Actor Jim Carrey is credited with having once written himself a check from an imaginary movie studio for the amount of money ($X millions) that in the future he planned to receive for starring in movies. After visualizing that amount over a period of time, according to the story, he now receives that amount for starring in each of his current movies.

The three major areas of your life that you may wish to focus on with your Treasure Map are:

1. Health
2. Wealth
3. Personal Happiness

The reason that this concept works so well, is simple. Most people learn and are motivated through visual means. By designing the Treasure Map, and then studying it carefully for a few minutes each day, you can stimulate your subconscious mind and imagination to generate creative ideas on how to solve your problems, accomplish you goals, and fulfill your dreams. But again...be specific!

"The me that I see, is the me that I'll be."
—Unknown Philosopher

REQUIREMENTS FOR SUCCESS

According to internationally renowned educator Steven A. Lavelle, there are three components that are essential if we are to accomplish any goal:

1. Desire

Before you're gonna, you gotta wanna. No one can force you to do anything against your will. No one can force you to be successful. Before you are going to succeed, you must first want to succeed.

2. Suspension of Disbelief

When you go to a movie, you don't actually believe what you see happening on the screen. But you don't dis-believe it either. So, you soon find yourself deeply engrossed in the movie. You laugh, you cry, your heart rate soars, your breathing becomes excited, your muscles grow tight...you suspended disbelief. In life, you don't actually have to believe in yourself or your ability to succeed, but you must allow yourself to not dis-believe it.

3. Dedication

Regardless of your circumstances, you must always remain determined to *"keep on keeping on"*—be dedicated to the accomplishment of your goals. I have a friend who told me once about his uncle, whom he considers to be a "loser". The uncle had made, and lost, 1 million dollars on 10 separate occasions. I pointed out that his uncle is not a loser. His uncle knows how to make the money, but he just doesn't know how to keep it. And if he keeps on trying, one day he will learn how to keep it, and will then suddenly become my friend's favorite uncle.

Sometimes we walk along a path beneath a cloudy sky,
There's nothing to the right or left to lift our spirits high...
Then, at last, we turn a corner and there bursts into our view,
A scene of light and beauty, and the world seems fresh and new.
So, always hold this little thought, that cares are bound to end.
And there's a brighter day ahead, just waiting 'round the bend.

—Unknown

GOAL EVALUATION

Finally, you must periodically evaluate your goals, based on their success and effectiveness, to determine if they should be continued, modified or eliminated, so that new goals and objectives can be created.

**"When I see a fence across my path,
I'll make a gate...or climb over...
But I'm going!"**
—Unknown

DREAM THE IMPOSSIBLE

Donna "Serious" Satchell—STARR Consulting & Training

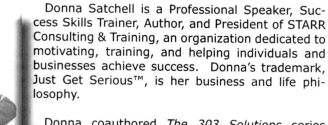

Donna Satchell is a Professional Speaker, Success Skills Trainer, Author, and President of STARR Consulting & Training, an organization dedicated to motivating, training, and helping individuals and businesses achieve success. Donna's trademark, Just Get Serious™, is her business and life philosophy.

Donna coauthored *The 303 Solutions* series which includes "quick read" books on time management, goal achievement, communication, and other topics. Along with Les Brown and Wally "Famous" Amos, and others Donna is featured in *The Power of Motivation*.

Prior to starting her business Donna worked at Clairol/Bristol-Myers. She became the first administrative assistant promoted into a management-level marketing position and was recognized as one of the company's experts on field-based analysis and category management. Donna graduated from college with top honors while working as an administrative assistant. A partial list of her clients include: The City of Atlanta, The Coca-Cola Company, Cox Enterprises, The Department of Labor, U.S. Small Business Administration, G.E. Consumer Finance and Centers for Disease Control (CDC), American Business Women's Association, International Association of Administrative Professionals, Clemson University's Conference for Women, and SCORE Conference for Women.

In 2000 Donna and colleague, Lynda Shorter, founded Women Aspiring Together To Succeed. Today, this group continues to motivate and empower women to grow in their awareness, understanding, and practice of self-care, self-empowerment, and self-achievement. Donna is a member of the American Society for Training & Development and the National Speakers Association (NSA). She is the past recipient of the NSA Georgia Chapter's Spirit Award for outstanding commitment and contribution. She serves on the Advisory Committee for DeKalb Technical College and is the 2008 - 2009 winner of "The Best Motivational Speaker in 5 Minutes or Less" and "The 2 Minute Adversity Challenge Speech", presented by The Twinkie Awards, which honors small business creativity and excellence.

STARR Consulting & Training
P.O. Box 870067 Stone Mountain, GA 30087
(770) 498-0400
www.JustGetSerious.com
donna@JustGetSerious.com

XIII.
Get Serious About Living Your Dreams:
Inside the Mind of Donna Satchell
Professional Speaker, Success Skills Trainer, Author

*"As an individual you have sit down and decide what
you want and how bad you want it. I believe that
most people really don't know what they want."*
—Donna *"Serious"* Satchell

Are you afraid of public speaking? If your answer is yes, then becoming a professional speaker might be the perfect dream for you. Well, that's how things worked out for Donna Satchell.

Almost twenty years ago she was an administrative assistant with no college degree, very little ambition, and a fear of public speaking. But starting and completing college in her mid-thirties left Donna with a craving for knowledge that has never been satisfied.

Today she is a top-notch speaker, trainer, and author who has shared the stage with the some of the best in the business, including Les Brown and yours truly, Al Duncan. Major corporations, small businesses, and government agencies know that when it's time to Just Get Serious™ about getting the results you want, it's time to call Donna *"Serious"* Satchell.

THE BIRTH OF BELIEF

How did you go from being an administrative assistant to a management level position in marketing to living your dreams?

I really thought I was going to be an administrative assistant my entire life. I didn't have any goals beyond that, but after ten years I was starting to get bored. At that time I was trying for a position that was titled Personnel Assistant [*not the same as a Personal Assistant*], but I couldn't get the position because I hadn't been to college.

I didn't think I was the smartest person in the world. I saw myself as being average, but I had this dream. First, I wanted to be a Personnel Assistant in human resources then I was going to work my way up. It was great to have the dream, but I didn't have what was required. So, that's how I started going to college.

Once you realize what is required to live your dreams, how do you begin to convince yourself to do what needs to be done?

Many times I think we don't move forward because we have these internal doubts and negative messages going on in our minds. And I think that continues throughout our lives. There are statistics that say for the average individual, 70%-80% of your thoughts are on the negative side of things.

So, you are sitting there with this goal or dream you know what's required and you're thinking, "I'm not smart enough." "I don't know the right people." "Someone like me will never get ahead." So, you have all of these negative things that you're buying into and then what happens is you get stuck. If you don't think you can do it, your friends are telling you can't do it, and you're looking at TV or magazines where everyone who does do it doesn't look like you or think like you or have the challenges you face, then it's easy to say, "I can't do it."

How you overcome that is by believing in yourself. You have to sit down and start to program your mind differently. You have to start investing in books and speakers you want hear because you have to reverse the message in your mind that's saying "you're not good enough" or any other negative message that's playing.

As an individual you have to sit down and decide what you want and how bad you want it. I believe that most people really don't know what they want.

Why don't people know?

They don't know because they haven't done it yet. We tend to live very limited lives. A couple of years ago I gave a presentation to a group of women who had all lived outside of the United States. Most of them were from Africa. They all had different types of careers and there was a vast array of experiences there. I had never thought of myself as living a limited life. It wasn't an "Oprah life", but I didn't see it as limited.

After the presentation one of them came up to me and asked, "What other countries have you lived in?" And I said, "I used to live in New York!"

Well, that is definitely another country!

They insisted that if I had the opportunity to do so, I should live in another country. That was a "Wow!" moment for me.

"You have to sit down and start to program your mind differently."

THE SPEAKER WHO WAS AFRAID TO SPEAK

When did you decide that you wanted speak for a living?

The way that happened was probably not the way it happened for most speakers. I had a huge fear of speaking. So, when I was working for Clairol, I also owned an art business at the time, and I was always taking public speaking classes because I didn't want to feel like I was going to pass out when I was giving a speech. I even joined Toastmaster's trying to get over the fear that I had.

The first time I did an Ice Breaker—which was my first speech— I was practicing my speech with Al Wiseman. He says to me, "Have you ever thought about being a speaker?" I thought that was the most bizarre thing. I would never want to do that in my life. It was like asking me out of the blue if I had ever thought about moving to Australia. I was looking at him as if he had said the craziest thing possible to me.

I didn't even think about what he said until six years later when I started a women's group with Linda Shorter. The group was focused on personal development. We had done several classes. We were the facilitators and I loved it, but we were doing it for free. So, I was trying to figure out how I could do that for a living. Then I remembered what Al Wiseman asked me. That's basically how I ended up becoming a professional speaker.

MICROWAVING YOUR DREAMS

What are some things that people do to impede their progress?

I think one thing that happens is they want it all right away. We live in a "microwave society". We have to realize that it's a journey, not a destination. If you find something you are passionate about then you don't mind the journey. When you love what you do, you love the process. You start seeing how you're changing and how you're opening up and how you're expanding yourself.

NEGATIVE THOUGHTS AND NEGATIVE FOLKS

The other thing is, as I mentioned earlier, the negativity. The thing about overcoming negativity is you don't just overcome it one time. You don't just join Negativity Anonymous and now you don't have to deal with that anymore. Negativity keeps showing up so you have to keep working on overcoming the negative thoughts.

When we get the negative people out of our lives we don't get them out one time. New people don't show up in our lives with a banner that says, "I'm negative! I am the negative one."

If only they did!

Every week I'm reading something motivational, something inspirational. I talk to people like you [Al Duncan]. Remember last time? We talked for two hours after your seminar on self-motivation.

Yes, indeed. Great conversation.

GET THE SKILLS, GET THE HELP

Maybe we don't have all the skills we need. If the dream isn't working maybe you aren't qualified right now. A couple of years ago I went and got some assistance, which I get on an on going basis now, from the SBDC [Small Business Development Center].

Step out of that comfort zone and do what you need to do. Sometimes people need to ask for help, but they don't want to ask for help. If you don't know the right people then start meeting new people.

One of the things I always recommend to people is to avoid "like me" networking. Don't have a group of friends or only network with people that are just like you. Interact with some other folks—some folks that are older or younger so that you have a new way of looking at life.

NO ENTHUSIASM, NO DREAM

I know that you feel like nothing great happens without enthusiasm so, touch on the importance of enthusiasm in this process.

You have to find a way to charge yourself up. The very first personal development book I read years ago was *Looking Out for Number One*. At that time I didn't even know there was a personal development section of the book store.

That's exactly how I was, too—didn't know a thing about personal development.

The only books I used to read were novels. I remember I was at a friend's house looking through his book case and he gave me *Looking Out for Number One*. As I read it I was like, "Wow!" All that talk about goals and dreams was new to me and it was very impactful.

One of the best ways to stay enthused is by listening to audio programs in the car. When I get into the car I know what I'm going to listen to. I'm going to spend that time getting enthused by listening to someone who is motivational, whoever it maybe. And you use that time to recharge yourself. If you listen to a lot of music, be careful because a lot of it is disempowering. When I was growing up all of the songs were about needing someone to love you. If you listened to that all the time then you started to feel that way.

**"Avoid 'like me' networking.
Don't have a group of friends or only network
with people that are just like you. Interact
with some other folks."**

KNOWLEDGE OF SELF

In order to stay motivated you're going to have to have a system in place. Find out what works for you. Life is not a one size fits all. You have to find out what motivates you and what demotivates you. It could be food. If you eat enough macaroni and cheese, fried chicken, and a milk shake, you are not going to do anything that afternoon!

Ha! Instead of working on your dreams you'll be snoring!

So, if that stuff slows you down and fogs up your thinking then you've got to stop doing it. Socrates said, "Know thyself."

And he got it from the Ancient Egyptians.

Oh. I carry that around in my wallet. "Know thyself." If you spend time knowing thyself then you start figuring all of this stuff out. But a lot of times we buy into other people telling us what we need to do, where we need to be, how we need to think, and we are not thinking for ourselves.

NO PROBLEMS?

Since you're a professional speaker many people think you're life must be easier because you teach all of this motivational stuff. What's the most challenging thing about being a professional speaker?

The most challenging thing for me was finding my direction. There are a lot ways to become a professional speaker. Whenever you're in a creative area where you don't have to go to school to get a degree there are a lot of different ways to do it.

So, you talk to this speaker and they're sending you in this direction. Then you talk to the next speaker and they're sending you in another direction. That might be okay when you're just exploring, but it can cause you to loose focus.

When I was working for Clairol I was dealing with the retail brand—Ms. Clairol. I was the assistant product manager. Every six months for 2 ½ years, they were changing managers. Every manager had a new direction for the brand. I remember thinking that it wasn't healthy for the brand.

That's what happened to me as a speaker. I kept changing directions and I didn't even realize I was doing it. Something told me that it would probably be better to go in one direction consistently—even if it might end being wrong later on—than to keep changing directions.

Everyone has advice. Everyone is telling you something different. I had to settle on a direction. Now I have a consultant down at the SBDC. This all goes back to knowing yourself because if you have a good sense of who you are then as you move forward and start being a speaker or whatever, you're going to draw on your own strength. Once you know who you are you'll start making better decisions.

GOTTA BELIEVE, GOTTA READ

I know you don't believe in regrets, but if there were one thing in your life you could've done differently what

would it be?

I would've started believing in myself and reading personal development books earlier. I probably would've gone to college earlier. I didn't go until I was around 34. College helped me to think and understand that there are different ways of thinking. When I was taking my courses they opened up the learning part of my mind. For years I told people that if I never get promoted it makes no difference. This whole experience of learning has been valuable to me.

The biggest challenge in my life right now is to always know what Donna believes. Just like everybody else, I'm constantly being influenced by people and the media, so I'm determined to separate it all so that I can know what I believe—so that I can know myself.

"A lot of times we buy into other people telling us what we need to do, where we need to be, how we need to think, and we are not thinking for ourselves."

XIV.
4 Questions to Help You Just Get Serious™ About Living Your Dreams

By Donna *"Serious"* Satchell

1. Do you know what you're passionate about? If you don't know, then get passionate about finding your passion.

Ask yourself what did I love to do when I was little? Start taking some classes, go to the museum or wherever. Start experimenting with life. Do new things. It doesn't have to take a whole lot of money to do. It may take a year or two or longer, but it doesn't matter because you're having fun with life. Enjoy the journey of finding out.

2. When are you going to start doing something? Commit to doing one small thing everyday.

For example, no matter what you want to do, there are people who are doing it and these people have an association that you may want to join. There are associations for everything. I invented a board game once. There's an Association of Board Game Inventors! If you can't find an association then go to the internet and find some people who are doing it. It's the starting that's hard.

A lot of times we're hesitant to ask people for help. If you want to write a book like Alice Walker then call Alice Walker or send her a letter. They say that there are six degrees of separation—we're only six people away from someone we want to know. Nowadays, I think it's more like two!

The way I hooked up with Les Brown [world renowned motivational speaker] is because one of my girlfriends met him in the airport. She new how excited I was about speaking—there's another reason to stay excited. So, when she ran into him at the airport she just started telling him all about me. "Oh my girlfriend wants to be a speaker just like you!" And he called me.

That was the most amazing thing. I came home and on my answering machine was a message from Les Brown! So, whatever you want to do talk to everybody about it.

3. What are your goals? You've got to write some goals.

These are the things that we already know. Write some goals and make sure you're moving forward on them. I'm a strong believer in treasure mapping—putting pictures of your dreams on boards. It's like a success collage to help keep you focused.

And make sure you goals are wide enough. You need goals for your career, for church, your family, relationships, or whatever.

4. How are you managing your time?

As you do things make sure you're asking yourself, "Why am I spending my time doing this?" "How does this support my goals and dreams?" The question I've heard asked is:

Are we driven by our dreams or driven by our distractions?

Many times we are driven by our distractions. You see an advertisement for Disney World and all of a sudden you're planning to go. Wait a minute. What happened to working on your dream?! Living your dreams and achieving your goals is all about time. We think it's about money. No. It's not all about money. It's about how you spend your time. If something doesn't support one of your goals then don't do it.

DARE TO

DREAM

XV.
The Difference Between a Man & a Male
A Special Message to Young Men
By Al Duncan

"What's the difference between a man and a male?"

I looked out at the lively group of several hundred young men at the Kansas Juvenile Correctional Complex and patiently waited for an answer. My question silenced the audience and a few seconds passed before I received an answer from a 16-year old in the middle of the crowd.

"Anybody can be a male, but it takes heart to be a man. A man ain't no coward! He don't show no fear."

With that answer the liveliness of the crowd returned in full force. I cracked a big grin and enjoyed every moment as they fired answers at me. Some raised their hands while others just shouted out their thoughts:

"A man takes responsibility, a male doesn't really care. He runs from his responsibility."

"A man can think for himself. He's got his own mind. He doesn't just blindly accept what people say."

"A male can have kids, but a man takes care of his kids."

"A man don't take no $#@! off of nobody!"

"Any male can have sex with female, but a man shows respect for his girl. If she's down with him, he's down with her."

"You are born a male. But I'm sayin', you gotta grow into bein' a man."

There were still dozens of young men, with their hands in the air, waiting for a chance to respond when someone sarcastically yelled, *"Why don't you tell us what the difference is?!"*

As all eyes honed in on me, the room grew silent again, and I began to share with them some of the things I'm getting ready to share with you.

THE DIFFERENCE

You can find a male almost anywhere. There are male lions and male whales; male butterflies and male spiders. There are even certain plants that are male. So, other than being in existence, it doesn't take much to be classified as a male. Being a man, however, is an entirely different story. Only a human being can become a man and only certain human beings become real men.

The answers that those young guys gave me at the Kansas Juvenile Correctional Complex are right to a certain degree, but some of those answers are based on ego and instinct. That's not always good.

instinct (in'stinkt') n. the natural, unreasoning, impulse by which an animal is guided to the performance of any action, without improvement in the method.

The difference between a man and a male is:

A man is the master of his instincts; a male is a slave to his instincts.

Duncan Nugget #407
A man uses his ability to THINK and
the Power of Choice to master his instincts.
A male is a slave to his instincts.

In other words, a real man can take control of his thoughts, emotions, and actions. He conquers his impulsive behavior. He is in charge of what he does and when he does it. He understands why he chose to do what he did. A male is just floating along like a feather in the wind. Anyone or anything can come along and blow him in any direction whatsoever and he has no idea where he will land.

INSTINCTS

Your instincts are normally controlled by your unconscious mind and therefore you are not always aware of them. In fact, mastering your instincts is a constant struggle even for real men because instincts are so powerful. They are always there waiting to take over in matters of life and death or in times of weakness.

Of all the living creatures on this planet, however, only human beings have the ability to think about and analyze their instincts. A man can THINK about what he's thinking about. He can THINK about how he's feeling. He can THINK about what he's doing while (or before) he's doing it and then choose to take a different course of action. This is known as *metacognition* (knowing/thinking about your thoughts) and *meta-mood* (knowing/thinking about your feelings and emotions).

The ability to THINK about your thoughts, emotions, and actions is the Power of Elevated (*Meta*) Consciousness. Combined with self-discipline, this power will allow you to master your mind.

Duncan Nugget #119
Master your mind; master your life.

TRAINING AND DEVELOPMENT

To a certain extent, people can train animals to go against their instincts. For instance, you could actually train a dog not to chase cats. Here's the interesting thing, however: under no circumstances could a dog train itself not to chase cats.

Only a human being can train and develop himself.

Training and developing yourself requires an elevated level of consciousness that should never be taken for granted because it gives you the power to create your world and live your dreams.

Without the ability to THINK and the Power of Choice you would be like any other creature on the planet—ruled by your instincts.

People and circumstances would have more control over your life than you do. Whatever life you start with would be the life you finish with. It would be the only life you could live. You could never really be more or have more. You would be at the mercy of anyone or anything that is fast enough, strong enough, or crafty enough to conquer, enslave, or eat you. THINK about that.

Million-Dollar Question:
Is that how you want to live
or
do you want to
take control of your life?

GOOD AND BAD

Before we continue, you should understand that *instincts aren't all bad.* Using your instincts can be a good idea because sometimes good instincts can save your life (like when you're walking down a dark street after midnight), help your performance (like when you're playing sports), or save you time and money (knowing when it's time sell a business or change careers). In other words, sometimes your gut feelings are right. But just as often, they are wrong—dead wrong. So...

YOU have to be the master of the situation, not your instincts.

Have you ever had a bad feeling about someone? Were you right? Maybe you were. But haven't you ever thought that someone wasn't cool and later on you found out that he or she was a lot cooler than you originally thought?

Haven't you ever had the feeling that you could really depend on someone, but later on he or she sold you out? Has something ever seemed like a great idea, but turned out to be a terrible idea?

In all of those cases your instincts were probably wrong and you had to pay the price. That's the problem with living life simply based on your instincts—it's a roll of the dice. You may get lucky for a while, but sooner or later relying solely on your instincts will probably get you into a jam. The world is too complex and fast moving to only live your life according to your instincts.

RUMBLE, RUN, OR THINK?

When an animal feels threatened (even if the threat isn't real) it will respond by attacking or running. That's called the Flight or Fight Response. It's a built in defense mechanism that all insects and animals (including humans) have. Unlike a male, a real man has the ability to rise above his initial Flight or Fight Response and choose his course of action.

A man can STOP and THINK. He can weigh the consequences of his actions and then make the CHOICE that he believes to be in his best interest and in the best interest of the people he cares about.

For example, in May of 2009 I was giving a keynote speech at Reynolds Community College in Richmond, Virginia. Prior to the keynote, I was leading a male empowerment session with some young men between the ages of 17 and 26. One of them, a 20-year old, told us a story about feeling like a chump.

He said that he was walking down the street and some dude was "grittin' on him". (When I was growing up in Philly that's what we called it when someone stares at you for no reason.)

"Mr. Duncan, he was staring at me like he wanted to do something. I felt like he was disrespecting me. I kept thinking that I should go over there and handle it, but I ain't got no time for that. I got things I'm tryin' to get done. I ain't got no time for the drama. I can't get no more strikes. But I felt like a coward, know what I'm sayin'?"

"You ain't no coward! That's just your pride talking," I responded. *"You weren't afraid of him. If you had to rumble with him you would have, right?"*

He smiled and nodded in agreement.

"But he wasn't threatening you, he was just grittin' on you. So, you didn't have to rumble. You thought about the situation and you chose to walk away because you didn't like the potential consequences. You have goals to accomplish and you decided that it wasn't worth it, right?"

"Yeah, I knew it wasn't worth it," he said with pride.

I gave him a *pound* (fist bump, some dap) and continued, *"That's what a real man does. He doesn't just blindly follow his instincts and emotions. He thinks and then he makes a choice. A real man is not a slave to his instincts or his ego."*

THE MALE EGO

The male ego is at the core of your instincts and when allowed to govern your life it is almost guaranteed to lead you to disaster. But let's be clear: there's nothing wrong with having confidence and pride about who you are. There's nothing wrong with having things that you absolutely will not put up with.

Duncan Nugget #408
When your male ego makes your view of a situation so foggy that it becomes impossible for you to see the consequences of your actions you are headed for trouble.

Think back to the story you just read about the young man in Richmond. How would you respond in a situation like that? It's a tough situation. When you feel threatened or disrespected, your instincts kick in—the Flight or Fight Response. Your instincts tell you that you need to handle it. You need to deal with it immediately, right?

Wrong.

What you immediately need to do is THINK. Get a clear understanding of what is going on and then use your Power of Choice.

If it's absolutely necessary, of course you have to stand up for yourself, your family, or your beliefs. Handle your business. That's what real men do. But FIRST...ask yourself:

Is it absolutely necessary?

Is this the best place and time to deal with the situation?

A man can THINK to himself:

"I'm not going to be disrespected, but I choose to handle this in a manner that won't create unnecessary drama. I refuse to do anything that's going to pull me off of my square, knock me out of the game, or keep me from accomplishing my goals."

WHAT IT IS AND ISN'T ABOUT

From business to athletics, politics to music, science to art, show me a **great** man from any walk of life and I'll show you a man that has, for the most part, mastered his instincts.

Mastering your instincts isn't about allowing people to disrespect you.

It's about knowing when it's better and more advantageous to walk away.

It's about being able to figure out if your behavior and actions are going to hurt you or help you.

It's about not allowing people and circumstances to pull you off of your square and knock you off of your path to success.

Mastering your instincts isn't about not having fun and not enjoying your life.

It's about overcoming laziness, procrastination, and stupid behavior so that you can live your dreams.

It's about diligence and self-discipline—doing what you need to do when you need to do it whether you feel like doing it or not.

It's about being able to enjoy life tomorrow because you took care of business and did the right thing today.

Mastering your instincts isn't about pretending to be someone else or not being true to yourself.

It's about the journey to becoming a better you.

It's about mastering the moment and defeating the enemy within you.

It's about refusing to allow negative environments, circumstances, and situations to define you.

REGARDLESS OF WHO YOU ARE...

While you are working on mastering you instincts, sometimes you can get beat up and beat down so much that you might actually begin to think that success and happiness are for everyone except you.

Garbage.

Sometimes you see more examples of people failing—people who look, act, and talk like you—than examples of people succeeding. If you aren't careful, you could begin to believe that mediocrity and being average is a part of every day life for you.

Garbage.

Sometimes, even when you think you are doing all the right things, it can seem like all the wrong things keep happening. Maybe that makes you start to think that after making so many mistakes, you are destined to be a failure.

Garbage.

Duncan Nugget #409
Regardless of your environment or circumstances; regardless of your situation or who you are, when you become the master of your instincts it is possible to live your dreams.

Tell me your problems and challenges and I'll show you someone with similar issues who has become successful.

Somewhere on this planet there's a success story about someone with a life similar to yours—someone who faced similar obstacles and challenges and if he or she made the CHOICE to succeed, so can you.

Duncan Nugget #124
Obstacles aren't reasons to fail.
They are reasons to succeed.

My grandmother used to always tell me, *"Al, you can't climb the smooth side of a mountain because there's nothing to hold on to. You've got to climb the rough side of the mountain."*

THINKING AIN'T EASY

Out of all the functions of your brain, thinking is by far the most taxing. Because it's so challenging and draining, people find a ridiculous amount of ways to avoid thinking.

For example, some people try to use drugs and alcohol to avoid thinking about their problems. That's too bad for them because if you don't take the time to THINK you will never rise above your circumstances. THINK about that.

Duncan Nugget #396
Your ability to THINK and the
Power of Choice are your super powers.
These powers enable you to shape
or change your circumstances
as well as your environment
instead of only being a product of
your circumstances and environment.

Quit making excuses to avoid thinking.

There's nothing wrong with watching TV and DVD's, catching up on your sleep, being on the internet, listening to music, or playing video games as long as you don't go overboard. In fact, relaxation and fun are good for your health. Just be careful because those things can become an excuse not to THINK.

Million-Dollar Question:
How often do you avoid thinking?

OVER-THINKING?

"But what if I THINK about things too much?"

Most people who ask me this question really do spend too much time thinking, but they're thinking about the wrong things. So, their thinking is completely unproductive.

They spend a lot of time thinking and agonizing over their problems instead of doing something about them. They spend too much time complaining to everybody they know about their problems instead of doing something about them.

Remember, thinking is not a replacement for taking the right actions, but the right kind of thinking is what helps you figure out the right actions to take. Make sure you:

- ✓ Invest more time in solving your problems than avoiding or over analyzing them. (Sometimes writing down the problem and the solution is helpful.)
- ✓ Invest more time in learning from your mistakes than repeating them.
- ✓ Invest more time in focusing on what you want instead of what you don't want.
- ✓ Invest more time in thinking than you do in zoning out.

HOW TO CHANGE YOUR LIFE

The Power of Choice is the steering wheel of your life.

If you want to steer your life in a different direction then make different choices. Yes, it really is that simple. The Power of Choice is the ultimate tool for changing your life. When you choose to do something, you take charge of your life. You didn't have to do it, you chose to do it. Nobody made you do it, you chose to do it.

That's power.

That's control.

That's freedom.

Duncan Nugget #171
Change your choices, change your life.

LIKE IT OR NOT, YOU HAVE ONE

"But what if I don't have a choice?"

Have you ever seen a movie called Bruce Almighty? In the movie, God (played by Morgan Freeman), gave Bruce (played by Jim Carrey) the power to be like God. Bruce could do absolutely anything he imagined. Well...almost anything. The one thing God would not allow him to do was mess with a person's Free Will. Even with all the power he had been given, Bruce could not take away a person's Power of Choice.

You have been blessed with the gift of **Free Will**. That means you always have a choice. Depending on your age and your situation, you might not have complete control over what's going on and you might not have much of a say-so about certain things but...

Duncan Nugget #172
You always have a choice.

You may not like your choices; nevertheless you always have at least two: do it (whatever it is) or don't do it; say it or don't say it; think it or don't think it. So, learn to say, "I choose to" instead of "I have to". People say things like:

"I have to go to school."

"I have to go to class."

"I have to go to work."

No you don't. Some people choose to go and some people choose not to go, right? One person says, "I'm going to class." The other says, "I'm skipping class." Both could have done the same thing, but one chose to go. That's because you don't have to do anything. THINK about that.

You are supposed to go to school.

You are supposed to go to class.

You are supposed to go to work.

You are supposed to pay your taxes.

You are supposed to obey the law.

You are supposed to do a lot of things, but you don't have to. You can THINK about the consequences and choose to do or not to do what you're supposed to do.

When you say "I chose to" or "I choose to" instead of "I had to" or "I have to" it helps you prove to yourself that YOU are in control of your life. This is a mind game that we are playing here and once you win this game you will realize that you have more control over your life then you may think you do. You have a choice and you should feel empowered because you have a choice.

Be proud when you choose to do what you are supposed to do. Get excited when you make choices that will lead to a better life. Know that if you made bad choices in the past starting right now you can choose to do better.

"I choose to go school."

"I choose to go to class."

"I choose to go to work."

If you used to say things like:

"He made me mad."

Now you can say:

"He didn't make me mad, I chose to get mad and if I want to, I can choose not to get mad."

In the past, if you chose to make excuses...if you chose not to take responsibility for your life...if you chose not to do the right things, you can choose to do something different—right now. You can choose take control of your life. **It's your choice.**

If you want to improve your life, make better choices. Make better choices than you've made in the past and make better choices than the unsuccessful people you come in contact with or hear about. And most importantly:

Avoid making the same stupid choices over and over

again.

IT'S NOT ABOUT WHAT YOU DON'T HAVE

If you are having a hard time believing that you always have a choice that's understandable because...

Sometimes what you don't have makes it hard to see what you do have.

Two of the young men that I mentor are twins named Justin and Jordan. (I know they're going to kill me for using their real names.) As of this writing, Justin and Jordan are 13 years old. They are smart, good-looking scholar-athletes. They get good grades and they're good basketball players. People that meet them can instantly tell that they've got a ridiculous amount of potential.

They're not perfect. They have a issues here and there. After all, boys will be boys, right? I'm not sure what career paths they will choose, but one thing is for sure: success is written all over their futures.

Justin and Jordan live with their mom, Nicole, who loves them more than anything in the world. Nicole is an attractive, hard-working single-mom of Trinidadian descent. She is full of passion and has a feisty, but loving personality. When she wakes up in the morning and goes to sleep at night the main thing on Nicole's mind is making sure her sons have every opportunity necessary for them to become successful.

Nicole has rules—strict rules. In other words, *"Mama don't play."* For example, no TV during the week and no phone calls after 9PM Monday thru Thursday. As you can probably imagine, rules like that lead to some interesting confrontations between the boys and their mother. Justin and Jordan love Nicole, but she drives them nuts. Of course, they drive her nuts, too. It's a typical I-love-you-but-I-can't-stand-you relationship between two teenage sons and a good mother.

It's always interesting talking to the twins because they love to talk to me about what they can't do. It's not the lack of

TV watching. That's been a part of their routine for years, so they don't really care about TV. It's things like not being able to go to the skating rink (at 10PM) with all of their friends or not being able to keep their mom from being what they consider to be over-protective.

If you looked closely, however, you would see that the twins get to do a lot. They play in basketball camps and tournaments all around the country. They wear the latest sneakers and nice clothes. They get to meet some of the most successful business people and professionals around. These are things that a lot of young people do not experience.

So, is Nicole over-protective or are the twins over-reacting? Who's right? Whose side am I on?

If those are the questions you are focused on then you are missing the point of what I'm teaching you. I'll tell you like I tell the twins:

Duncan Nugget #175
Focus on the choices you have not on the ones you don't.

A lot of times it might seem like someone is always bossing you around or making your choices for you—parents, teachers, professors, managers, supervisors, the police, the government, superior officers, and I'm sure you can think of more. If someone is actually bossing you around, you have to figure out how you are going to deal with it in an effective and productive manner.

Life is extremely frustrating when you only focus on what you don't have and what you can't do. Too many people waste their time complaining about the choices and options that they don't have.

They use what they don't have and what they can't do as excuses not to do what they can do.

They come up with a ton of reasons to make poor choices.

For instance, you could be upset about where you live or you could be mad because you don't see a whole lot of opportunity around you. So, you could use the limited choices in front of you as an excuse to say, "What's the point? I can't find a job, school costs too much, and life sucks, so to hell with everybody and everything."

Garbage.

Only a weak male would think like that. A real man understands this nugget right here:

Duncan Nugget #174
The choices you make today determine the choices you'll face tomorrow.
If your choices are limited at the moment, that is no excuse to ruin your choices in the future.

The choices you make in the present decrease or increase the choices you will have in the future. Smart choices produce more options and opportunities. Stupid choices destroy your options and opportunities.

The lesson for the twins and YOU is simple. Everybody has things they wish they could do. There are choices and options that we all wish we had. The only way to change that is to maximize the choices and opportunities you have now because that's how you end up with more choices and opportunities in the future. THINK about that.

Imagine walking through a maze. When you make the right turn, you can keep moving. Make the wrong turn and you hit a dead end. It works the same way in life. If you make the right choices now, sooner or later you'll escape the maze of misery. Sooner or later you will have a choice about where you live. Sooner or later you will have a choice about where you want to go to school, where you work, how much money you plan to make, the kind of clothes you want to wear, and who you allow to be a part of your life. It all begins and ends with a choice.

But You Do Have a Choice...

"I'm only 17 and I live with my parents. I don't have a choice about where I live."

But you do have a choice about how hard you work in school and/or on your job so that you can live where you want to in the future. You do have a choice about how many books you read in order to become a better man.

"I'm 24 and I don't have a lot of experience or money so, I don't have a choice about where I work."

But you do have a choice about how well you do your job when you get one, whatever it may be. You do have a choice about how you save or invest your money so that eventually you can go to school and get a better job or start your own business.

"I'm a senior in high school and I don't get along with my teacher. I don't have a choice about who my teacher is."

But you do have a choice about finding a mentor or asking for someone for help. You do have a choice about having a positive or negative attitude. You do have a choice about doing what you have to do so that you can pass that class and never have to deal with that teacher again.

You do have a choice.

Million-Dollar Question:
How can you make the most out of the choices and options you have right now?

THE "R" WORD

"With great power comes great responsibility."

—Spider-Man, 2002

Far too many people give away their Power of Choice because they are afraid of dealing with the "R" word—responsibility. A real man embraces the Power of Choice and the responsibility that comes with it. He uses it to his advantage at all times.

The reason that leaders like CEO's, officers in the armed forces, business owners, and presidents get more money and recognition is because they take on the most responsibility. So, realize that responsibility is nothing to be afraid of; it's something for which you should be thankful. If somebody else is responsible for your life doesn't that mean that someone else is in control of your life?

Do you really want somebody else to be in control of your life?

Responsibility isn't always easy to deal with. Sometimes it's very frustrating to look at your life and realize that there's no one to blame except for the man in the mirror.

In The Mirror

"I can't believe you did this to me", says the guy.

"I only did what you told me to do," says his reflection.

While I was writing this, I took a break to reflect on what I wanted to say. During my break I checked my Facebook page. Guess what people were chatting about. That's right—choices. As I read through the comments I came up with another nugget:

Duncan Nugget #494
In life you either
choose to accept things as they are
or
you choose to accept responsibility
for changing them.

CONSEQUENCES AND RIPPLE EFFECTS

The Power of Choice operates under the Principle of Cause and Effect:

**"Every cause has its effect and
every effect has its cause."**

Choices are causes that produce effects (consequences) therefore every choice ends with a consequence and every consequence started with a choice.

Duncan Nugget #173
You can control your choices,
but not the consequences.

You know what it looks like when someone throws a pebble in a pond, don't you? Once you throw the pebble (a choice) and the ripples start (the consequences) you can't stop them. The only way to change the ripples (and you still can't completely stop them) is to throw another pebble or something else (a different choice) into the pond which will start to produce a different set of ripples (new consequences).

This is why making a choice is so powerful. After a few bad choices you could have all kinds of negative ripple effects—which you have no control over—going on in your life. The cool thing is: it works the other way, too. A few good choices and you could have all kinds of positive ripple effects—which you have no control over—going on in your life.

Variations of Cause and Effect

"You reap what you sow."

"To every action there is an equal and opposite reaction."

"What goes around, comes around."

AWARENESS & SELF-DISCIPLINE

Awareness is the key. Unfortunately, most people only become aware of the consequences after they make the choice. As a result, they end up in places and situations that are far away from where they dreamed they would be.

Duncan Nugget #180
The person who can clearly see the consequences of his choices before he makes them is a person of great wisdom and power.

Have you ever asked yourself or somebody else, *"Why would you do something so stupid?"* Some of the typical responses are:

"I don't know what I was thinking."

"I have no idea."

"I didn't know it was going to turn out like that."

"It seemed like a good idea at the time."

Duncan Nugget #126
True awareness and stupidity seldom hang out together.

Most of the time, when people do stupid, impulsive things, they are not truly aware of the potential consequences. But sometimes, however, people know the potential consequences and for some reason, they make dumb choices anyway. They think to themselves, *"That's what happened to everybody else, but it won't happen to me."* A little while later, it's those same people who are saying, *"I didn't know it was going to turn out like that."*

Understand that impulsive behavior, which is a lack of self-discipline, is one of the main causes of mistakes—especially big mistakes. When you lack self-discipline you make choices without stopping to THINK or taking the time to get the right information you need to make a good choice. The consequences can be disastrous.

Duncan Nugget #127
No self-discipline; no success.
Self-discipline is the secret weapon of the master. It keeps your instincts in check. It keeps you striving. It helps to keep temporary fun from turning in to permanent consequences.

Self-discipline is the best way to increase your awareness because it helps you to stop and THINK. It helps you make the time to become more aware of the potential consequences of your choices. Self-discipline helps you realize that just because it feels good doesn't mean that it is good.

The more you have the discipline to THINK before you act the better you will become at seeing the potential consequences. The more you learn from your mistakes *and the mistakes of other people* the better you will become at seeing the potential consequences.

QUIT CRYING & MAN UP

"But what if the right choice turns out to be wrong choice?"

Then quit "boo-hooing", get yourself together, and get to work. This is where real men choose to man up because...

Duncan Nugget #21
Failure is only permanent if you quit.

Read that nugget again. Almost any time I have a speaking gig or if I'm mentoring someone, that phrase will come out of my mouth. It's also in many of my articles and books.

People tend to think that phrase is supposed to get them motivated or give them the determination and persistence they need to succeed. Actually, the main purpose of that phrase is to weed out worry and help you conquer the fear of failure. Failure is only a phase. Failure is feedback about the choices you've made. In order to stay in "failure mode" a person would have to quit getting better. He would have to give up on pursing his dreams and becoming successful.

Speaking of success, let's be clear about something:

Duncan Nugget #22
Success is only permanent if you keep striving.

Nobody gets it right all the time. Muhammad Ali didn't land every punch. Einstein didn't have all the answers. Tiger Woods doesn't always make par. Donald Trump doesn't make money on every deal. Will Smith isn't always in a blockbuster. George Lopez doesn't always get a laugh. Jay-Z doesn't always go triple platinum. I'm a professional speaker, but my words don't always come out perfectly. Great men make mistakes, but they learn to take the time to THINK before they act and then make the best choice they can. Just like other real men, you won't get every choice right. That's okay. There's no need to worry or be afraid.

Just get better.

Do better.

THINK about your choices and the consequences then take the right action. It doesn't matter who your hero is, he (or she) has flaws like everyone else, but flaws can be minimized by mastering your instincts.

PAY THE PRICE

"Mr. Duncan, I've applied for like a hundred jobs. What am I supposed to do?" I could see the frustration on Corey's face. He was tired of the rejections.

"You keep tellin' me failure is only permanent if I quit. I don't want to quit, but this is getting ridiculous. I gotta eat," he continued.

"I gotta eat" was his way of saying he might have to do something illegal...again. Corey is a 22-yr old convicted felon. Selling drugs to make ends meet (and get women) nearly ruined his life, but he finally got his GED. He's even working on going to a technical school, but he needs money.

"I don't want to hear it, Corey," I responded. *"You messed up. Now man up and pay the price. Of course, it's harder for you to get a job. You're a convicted felon, but I know you can do this."*

"Come on Mr. Duncan! I did my time."

"Look, man. Let me tell you something. You still gotta reap what you sow. That's cause and effect. You gotta plant some new seeds and give them time to grow."

"So what am I supposed to do?"

"Apply for another hundred jobs."

"What?!"

I didn't respond. I just looked at Corey. Finally he asked, *"Do you really think somebody is going to hire me?"*

"Eventually somebody will. You just have to accept the fact that you made some mistakes and that's going to cost you. But it won't stop you. Nothing can stop you except for who?"

Corey nodded his head, gave me a pound, and walked off.

Three weeks later he had a job. A year later he was in school to become an electrician.

There is a price to be paid for making the wrong choices.

The bigger the mistake, the higher the price.

That's life.

Don't be mad because there's a price. Be glad for the opportunity to make your life better. Be thankful for the opportunity to plant new seeds. Be grateful that failure is only permanent if you quit. **Pay the price and get on with your life.**

THINKING WITH YOUR LITTLE HEAD OR YOUR BIG HEAD?

There is no way we could talk about male instincts without talking about sex. It is one of the three strongest instincts that humans have (hunger, fear, and sex/reproduction). The desire for sex can turn a smart man into an idiot. On the other hand, it can turn a coward into a fearless warrior.

People do crazy things in the name of lust and love.

There are few things that can ruin your life faster than having sex with the wrong person at the wrong time. I'm not going to give you a lecture about sex, but I will say that you need to do a good deal of thinking about where you stick your penis.

The consequences can be devastating.

The ripple effects are never-ending.

The price you have to pay is HIGH.

Some of the most successful men in history have been ruined because they couldn't keep it in their pants. Make sure that's not you.

Duncan Nugget #406
If more males were as dedicated
to chasing their dreams as they are
to chasing females the results
would be amazing.

MAKING BETTER ONES

We've spent all this time talking about choices. Aren't you wondering if there is a way to make better choices? Well, there is. Remember what I said previously—there's no way to get it right all the time, but here are five tips to help you make better choices.

5 Tips for Making Better Choices

1. Get the right info.

Having the right info is the most important part of making the right choice. Every now and then you might get lucky, but normally the wrong info will lead to the wrong choice. Keep reading and studying books like this one as well as books, magazines, and whatever else you can find that will give you the knowledge to make yourself better. Make it your business to know the people with the right info.

2. Pause and THINK.

There is no right or wrong answer on how long to pause, but I suggest that you pause long enough to make sure you have the right info and a good understanding of the possible consequences (positive and negative).

3. Think on paper.

Sometimes when you have a tough choice to make, it's easier if you put things in writing. Get a piece of paper and draw a line straight down the middle. On one side, write down what will happen once you make the choice. On the other side, write what will happen if you don't make the choice. This exercise will help you to see the possible consequences of your choice.

4. Focus on what's important.

Keep in mind the goals you want to accomplish and what's most important in your life. NEVER let your choices push you further away from your goals and your priorities. Your choices should move you closer to what's important in your life and move you further away from problems and situations you want to avoid.

5. Get some help.

If it's a really tough choice get some advice from a mentor or someone that's an expert at whatever type of choice you have to make. Just be sure that whoever you are getting help from knows his or her stuff. Bad advice is worse than no advice.

WHO'S THE MAN?

Million-Dollar Question:
Are you a man?

Be careful about answering that question too quickly. Males love to claim, "I'm a man!", but as you learned while reading this book:

It takes a lot more than words to be a man.

Doing what's required to be a real man—a great man—is hard work and it can be a heavy burden. But if you use the wisdom you gained while reading this, I know you can carry the load because...

You're the man!

I am a man.

Regardless of my circumstances,
it is possible for me to live my dreams.

I have the ultimate tools at my disposal:
the ability to THINK and the Power of Choice.

With these tools in my arsenal
the only person that can stop me is me
and I refuse to lose.

I choose
to learn what I need to know
to get where I want to go.

I choose
to use my knowledge to improve my life
and the lives of others.

I choose
to take care of my health
and build wealth.

I choose
to embrace my responsibilities,
not run from them.

I choose
to be the master of my instincts,
not a slave to them.

I choose
to be a man.

—Al Duncan

Bibliography

Allen, James. *As a Man Thinketh.* 1902

Carnegie, Dale. *How to Win Friends and Influence People.* 1936. Revised edition. New York: Pocket Books, 1981.

Chu, Chin-Ning. *Thick Face, Black Heart: Thriving, Winning, and Succeeding in Life's Every Endeavor.* Antioch, California: AMC Publishing, 1992

Duncan, Al. *My Success Journal For Young People (3rd Edition).* Atlanta, Georgia: Al Duncan Publishing, 2011.

Gladwell, Malcolm. *The Tipping Point: How Little Things Can Make a Big Difference.* 2000. New York: Back Bay Books/Little, Brown, and Company, 2002.

Goleman, Daniel. *Emotional Intelligence: Why It Can Matter More Than IQ.* New York: Bantam Books, 1995.

Hill, Napoleon. *Think and Grow Rich.* 1937 (Public Domain)

Hogan, Kevin. *The Psychology of Persuasion: How to Win Others to Your Way of Thinking.* Gretna, Louisiana: Pelican Publishing, 1996.

Kimbro, Dennis. Hill, Napoleon. *Think and Grow Rich: A Black Choice.* New York: Fawcett Books, 1991.

Maltz, Maxwell. *Psyco-Cybernetics: A New Way to Get More Living Out of Life.* North Hollywood, California: Wishire Book Co., 1973

Mandino, Og. *The Greatest Salesman in the World.* Hollywood, Florida: Frederick Fell, 1968.

Robbins, Anthony. *Unlimited Power.* New York: Fawcett, 1987

Trine, Ralph Waldo. *In Tune With the Infinite.* 1897. (Public Domain)

Tzu, Sun. *The Art of War.* Translated by Thomas Cleary. Boston, Massachusetts: Shambala Publications, 1988.

Other books by Al Duncan:

Big Money Student™:
21 Easy Ways to Make An Extra
$1000 This Semester
(April 2011)

Reach Your Potential:
Turning Your Unlimited Potential
Into Peak Performance
Coming soon! Summer 2011

Also available:

My Success Journal
For Young People (3rd Edition)

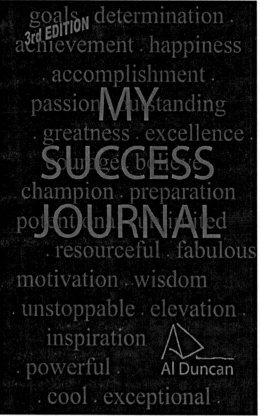

THIS IS NO
ORDINARY JOURNAL.

It is a well known fact that if you want to be successful you should write down your goals and how you plan to accomplish them. And now young people have a special place to do it...
in their personal success journal.

My Success Journal For Young People (3rd Edition) is full of empowering *Duncan Nuggets™ for Your Noggin*—articles, tips, quotes, and engaging exercises on:

✓ Understanding the REAL definition of success

✓ Goal *getting*

✓ Overcoming failure

✓ Conquering your fears

✓ Building self-confidence and self-discipline

✓ Dealing with haters and doubters

✓ Developing your strengths and managing weaknesses

✓ Creating a strong personal brand

✓ Avoiding the potential pitfalls of social media

✓ How to be more successful NOW.

✓ ...and more!

Al Duncan is the leading motivational speaker for at—risk youth and troubled young people. An internationally recognized authority on youth development and empowerment, Al has delivered **Duncan Nuggets™** live and in-person to over one million young people around the world.

He is the founder of **YoungScribes™**, a fundraising program that allows schools and youth organizations to publish books, written by their young people, for free. Al is the author of **My Success Journal For Young People, Get ALL Fired Up!**, **Big Money Student™** and his latest book, **Reach Your Potential.** (Al Duncan Publishing, Summer 2011.) He has been awarded the President's Call to Service Award and The National PTA Life Achievement Award, for his outstanding service in the field of youth development and empowerment.

Al was born and raised in one of the most dangerous neighborhoods on the planet in North Philadelphia and by today's standards, would've been labeled an "at-risk" student. When he was 5 years old he was molested by a male friend of the family. Emotionally traumatized, it took him years to remember what happened. At the age of 15, Al's world was torn to shreds again when he found out that his father, his childhood hero, was addicted to crack cocaine.

Devastated, but not defeated, Al refused to allow his personal problems stop him. He went on to enjoy careers as a professional saxophone player and a professional chef. His father's struggle and incredible recovery inspired Al to write *Duncan Nugget™ #21:* Failure is only permanent if you quit.

At the age of 24, he walked away from his musical career and took on the tremendous responsibility of raising his youngest brother who was 12 years old at the time. Today, as a tireless advocate for youth development and empowerment, Al is a high energy, high content, high impact speaker, lecturer, and motivational powerhouse.

Have you been getting your **Duncan Nuggets™**?
Get'em for FREE at **www.alduncan.net**

Al Duncan
*"The World's Leading Speaker for At-Risk
and Troubled Young People"*

High Energy!   High Content!   High Impact!

Assemblies
Conferences
Orientation
Commencement
Convocations
Leadership Retreats
Diversity Events
Black History Month
Greek Life
Workshops
Moderator/Emcee
Panel Discussions
Student Government Events
PTA/PTSA

**Book Al Today!
1-888-810-4302
speaker@alduncan.net
www.alduncan.net**

Partial Client List:
U.S. Department of Education
National Guard - Army Reserve - Department of Justice
The Ontario Ministry of Children & Youth Services
Workforce Development - University of Georgia
Spelman College - Morehouse College - FCCLA
Milton Hershey School - NASC - Georgia Tech
University of Connecticut - Johnson & Wales University
Georgia Adult Education Association
Claflin University - South Carolina State University
Clark Atlanta University - University of Northern Iowa
Department of Juvenile Justice - Job Corps
Hundreds of Colleges, High Schools, Middles Schools

CPSIA information can be obtained at www.ICGtesting.com
Printed in the USA
LVOW031917210911

247318LV00001B/3/P